ARCHAEOLOGY AND THE BIBLE

ARCHAEOLOGY AND THE BIBLE

BILL HUMBLE

Christian Communications
P.O. Box 150
Nashville, Tennessee 37202

Photographs are by Bill Humble. Used by permission.

Published by Christian Communications
A division of the Gospel Advocate Co.
P.O. Box 150, Nashville, TN 37202

ISBN 0-89225-370-3

CONTENTS

CHAPTER ONE

The Old Testament

Bill Humble:

The Old Testament is a book of history. Beginning in Genesis 12, it tells the story of Abraham and Sarah who lived nearly 4,000 years ago. And the rest of the Old Testament is the story of their descendants, the people of Israel, how they settled in this land and how they lived in war and peace with the nations around them — Syria, Egypt and Babylon. The Old Testament tells about real people, real places, and real events from the ancient past.

Archaeology also deals with the past, and over the last hundred years, archaeology has been of great value in bringing the world of the Bible to light. As archaeologists have excavated here in the Bible world, cities and whole civilizations have emerged from the past. And the more we can learn about those ancient people — their languages and culture and way of life — the better we can understand the Bible.

As archaeologists began work here in the Bible land about 100 years ago, they found that ancient cities were built on hills called tells. The reason for this was that a city on a hill was easier to defend.

Here, for example, is the tell of ancient Hazor, a town that Joshua captured and destroyed.

Tell el Hesi is the site where real archaeology began in the Bible land. Sir Flinders Petrie, an Englishman, began excavations here in 1890 and became the father of biblical archaeology. Petrie formulated the two principles that have guided archaeology ever since. First, these tells have strata, the ruins of different levels of civilization lying on top of one another like layers of a cake. Second, broken pottery, that is found everywhere, is the key to dating the different levels.

Tell el Hesi is located on the Philistine plain, where Israel struggled with the Philistines for centuries.

At Lachish, also near the Philistine plain, Joseph Shulam explains how tells are formed:

Joseph Shulam:

Lachish is a tell and it is a tell that has about 13 different civilizations that have come and settled on top of each other. Sometimes the city was burned like in the days of Joshua, that is described in the book of Joshua, and leaves a layer of black soot that is very visible when you see that the archaeologists have come and dug a straight shaft through the tell like through a cake. There they are able to read the civilization like they read the layers of a cake.

Bill Humble:

Notice level nine. These ashes are from the Canaanite city that Joshua burned about 1300 B.C.

But let's go back to the days of Abraham and Sarah, who lived nearly 4,000 years ago. Abraham spent most of his life as a Bedouin wandering with his flocks here in the hill country of Judaea around Hebron and Beersheba.

But Abraham came to this land from Ur of the Chaldees, a thousand miles to the east in modern Iraq. Ur was excavated in the 1920s by Leonard Wooley. He found a pyramid, called a ziggurat, built long before Abraham. It's been restored. He also found a royal tomb with some beautiful treasures in it.

One is the "Standards of Ur" — little figures made of white seashell set in a background of blue stone. It's a panorama of war and peace: Soldiers and chariots march off to war. And after the victory they celebrate with a feast. A bullock is about to be sacrificed. And notice the musician playing on a lyre.

Tomb of Patriarchs at Hebron covers the Cave of Machpelah.

Archaeologists found a lyre like this at Ur, shaped like a bull, and overlaid with gold. It is several hundred years older than the time of Abraham.

After Abraham left Ur and came into the Bible land, he lived as a Bedouin, wandering over the Judaean hills with his flocks. When we visit a Bedouin tent today, we see a way of life that is almost unchanged from the days of Abraham. And we might be looking into the face of Abraham.

The Tomb of the Patriarchs is built over the Cave of Machpelah. When Sarah died, Abraham purchased the Cave of Machpelah from Ephron the Hittite. Sarah was buried here in the cave, later Abraham, then Isaac and Rebecca.

Then, in the years just before Jesus was born, Herod the Great built these massive walls around the site. This is typical Herodian construction, and it is the largest Herodian building still standing in the Bible land. Notice the stonework with a marginal draft around each stone. We'll see the same kind of stonework around the temple mount in Jerusalem.

The Tomb of the Patriarchs has been a Muslim shrine since the seventh century, so no archaeological work is allowed here, and we have no idea what might be found in the cave.

Here's another site that may be connected with Abraham. Genesis 13 tells how Abraham came and pitched his tent by the oaks of Mamre at Hebron, and most scholars believe this is the site of the oaks of Mamre. There's an ancient well here, and some believe it was dug by Abraham.

Herod the Great built a wall enclosing the area. Some of these stones have the margin around them like other Herodian buildings.

Then, in the fourth century, the emperor Constantine built a large church here with Abraham's oak in the atrium. Many of these ruins are of that church.

Three generations after Abraham, his family went down into Egypt. They followed an ancient road, the Way of the Sea, that is still traveled today.

We have evidence that Semitic people often migrated to Egypt in time of famine. Archaeologists have found a tomb painting at Beni Hasan showing 34 Semitic people coming into Egypt. They are led by a man named Abishar. The men carry weapons and musical instruments, and they are followed by the women and children. Entering Egypt — 200 or 300 years before Jacob and Joseph.

The next chapter in Old Testament history is the Exodus from Egypt and the conquest of the land — beginning here at Jericho.

Joseph Shulam:

We are here at the old Roman road that used to lead into Jericho through the Wadi Qilt, and as you can see, we are in the Judaea desert still, but looking toward Jericho, which is the largest oasis in the Middle East. That's why it became one of the most popular sites in ancient times and also in modern time, and it is the oldest city that archaeologists have discovered in civilization — 7,000 B.C.

Bill Humble:

There have been extensive excavations in the tell of Jericho over the past 50 years. Archaeologists have found the old city wall that goes back to around 2000 B.C. Sun-dried mud bricks can still be seen in the walls.

John Garstang worked at Jericho in the 1930's, and Garstang believed that he had found the walls from Joshua's day — the walls that fell down when Israel marched around the city. But later archaeologists, like Kathleen Kenyon, have decided that Garstang's dating was wrong and that the walls from Joshua's time have not been found.

One of the most important discoveries at Jericho is a stone tower that is more than 20 feet tall. The tower is buried deep in the heart of the tell, and this shows that it was built around 7000 B.C. What was the tower used for? Archaeologists are not sure.

Joseph Shulam:

The tower could have been for a fortification or could have been as a type of ziggurat, a holy site, a place of worship for some Canaanite deity. But it is recorded here that there were already community projects at 7000 B.C., which makes Jericho the oldest city in human civilization.

Bill Humble:

The Israel Museum has some beautiful pieces of art from Jericho. This is the head of a statue that Garstang found, and it goes back to about 6000 B.C., nearly as old as the tower.

Garstang also found this vase with a human face, and the sharp nose and chin. It was made about 1600 B.C. The Israel Museum calls it a "masterpiece of Canaanite art," and it shows the high level of civilization in the land before the conquest.

After Jericho Joshua marched north and attacked Hazor. Hazor is the largest tell anywhere in the Bible land, and it had been the most important Canaanite city in the north for 500 years. It was even protected by a moat around the tell. But according to Joshua 11, the Israelites captured Hazor and burned it, and archaeologists have confirmed that destruction in the 13th century B.C.

Three hundred years later, Solomon rebuilt Hazor and made it one of his three chariot cities. Archaeologists have found the city gate of Solomon's city with its six chambers, and they have found a casement wall. A casement wall is a double wall, much stronger than a single wall.

Later kings, like Ahab, continued building Hazor. Here is a large storage area, with standing pillars, from the days of Ahab.

The ancient water system at Hazor was discovered by Yigael Yadin in 1968. Yadin found a vertical shaft 90 feet deep, and at the bottom of the shaft, a sloping tunnel 75 feet long that went down to the natural underground springs. This insured that Hazor had a water supply, and it shows that Hazor was an important city guarding Israel's northern border in the days of Omri and Ahab.

Megiddo is one of the most important archaeological sites from Old Testament times. This was a Canaanite royal city, 2000 B.C., captured by the Israelites, then rebuilt and fortified by Solomon to be one of his chariot cities.

Megiddo had a strategic location in the Valley of Jezreel, or Megiddo, and it controlled the Way of the Sea, the most important trade route through the Bible land.

Elias Subeh of Bethlehem has been a guide in the Bible land for 40 years, and he talks about Megiddo's importance.

Elias Subeh:

Megiddo is one of the Canaanite royal cities located on a crossroad, and it was a very, very important city in the early days, especially for the caravans passing by.

Bill Humble:

Megiddo was excavated by the University of Chicago in the 1930s. They cut a deep trench through the tell and identified at least 20 different levels of civilization.

Here is a large Canaanite altar, built around 2500 B.C. and used for animal sacrifice. Nearby you can see the foundations of a Canaanite temple.

According to 1 Kings, Solomon rebuilt Megiddo as one of his chariot cities. Here's his city gate on the north side of the city. Solomon also built stables for the horses, and many stone mangers can still be seen among the ruins.

Elias, what's this you're sitting on?

Elias Subeh:

This is the stables where the 450 horses were kept, and this is what we call a stone manger. It will explain the way the Lord was laid in a manger in Bethlehem. That's where they used to put the chaff, and here is the ring where they used to tie the horse. So this is a stone manger found in the city of chariots of Solomon.

Bill Humble:

There was a large grain silo near the stables. We can still see the ancient steps leading down to the bottom of the silo.

Megiddo also had a large tunnel to provide a water supply in time of siege. First, they dug a vertical shaft 90 feet deep down through the tell. The ancient steps going down the shaft can still be seen. Then a tunnel over 200 feet long was cut through the rock to a spring outside the tell. Finally, the spring was covered and concealed, so the only access to the water was from inside the city.

Here's a beautiful piece of Canaanite art found here at Megiddo. It's done on ivory, and it shows a Canaanite king, maybe the king of Megiddo, sitting on his throne. He holds a cup and a lotus blossom. The queen stands before the throne along with a musician playing a lyre. One of the king's soldiers brings two prisoners before him. They are naked, and they are circumcised.

The ivory goes back to about 1200 B.C., so it may be a picture of one little Canaanite victory during Israel's conquest of their land.

Following the conquest and the judges, the Old Testament story turns to David and Solomon and the temple in Jerusalem.

Let me tell you about a treasure from Solomon's temple that has recently been discovered. Jerusalem remained a foreign Jebusite city here in the Bible land 'til the days of David when it was captured by David about 1000 B.C. Then his son Solomon built the temple here on Mt. Moriah where the Dome of the Rock stands today. The Dome is a Muslim shrine, and no archaeological work is allowed on the temple mount. So we have no idea what remains of Solomon's temple might survive underground.

But recently a small pomegranate made of ivory was discovered. The little pomegranate has an inscription in archaic Hebrew, and it says, "Belonging to the temple of the Lord, holy to the priests." Scholars believe that this pomegranate was a decoration on the top of a scepter that priests carried in the temple. If so, it's a priceless treasure. It's the only artifact from Solomon's temple that has ever been discovered.

But as archaeologist John Wilson points out, many discoveries in the Bible land, like this pomegranate, show that the Bible tells about real people and real places.

John Wilson:

When we start a fairy tale, we say, "Once upon a time in a far-away land, there lived a king." But we know that is not a real place or a real king. You come to Israel, you dig, and you find things King Herod built. You find inscriptions with his name on them or some other king from Bible times. You know you are not dealing with fairy tales; you are dealing with real people, with real events. To me, that is the major value of archaeology. It gives us a context of reality around the spiritual truths of the Bible.

Bill Humble:

As we think about archaeological discoveries that relate to the Old Testament, we can see at least three ways that archaeology can be of value in studying the Bible.

First, archaeology gives us a picture-window into the ancient world. It shows us how people lived in the days of Abraham and David.

Second, archaeology helps us understand the Bible, for the more we know about the ancient world, the better we can understand every biblical event that happened in that world.

Third, discoveries of archaeology have sometimes confirmed the historical accuracy of the Bible in very specific ways.

Scriptures for Study

Genesis 11:27-32. Abraham leaves Ur.

Genesis 13:18; 18:1-21. Oaks of Mamre at Hebron.

Genesis 23:1-20. Cave of Machpelah.

Joshua 6:1-27. Conquest of Jericho.
Joshua 11:1-15. Capture of Hazor.
1 Kings 9:15-22. Solomon's chariot cities.

Notes from Archaeology

Excavations at Ur

The ruins of Ur of the Chaldees are located on the Euphrates River in southern Iraq, not far from where many bitter battles were fought in the recent Iraq-Iran War. Ur is mentioned four times in the Old Testament: Genesis 11:28,31; Genesis 15:7; and Nehemiah 9:7.

Ur was first excavated by J.E. Taylor in the 1850s under the auspices of the British Museum. But the major work came in the early 20th century (1922-1934) when Sir Leonard Wooley worked at Ur with the support of the Museum and the University of Pennsylvania. Wooley showed that Ur was inhabited from 4000 B.C. until 300 B.C., and that the city's history reflects the development of Sumerian culture.

One of the most important discoveries was the ziggurat of Ur, built by King Ur-Nammu about 2100 B.C. The "ziggurat" is a Mesopotamian pyramid, different from the pyramids of Egypt in that it was built in a series of steps or terraces. The ziggurat at Ur was a shrine to the moon god, and its base was 200 by 170 feet. It was covered with blue glazed tiles, and there were gardens of tress and shrubs on the terraces. The biblical Tower of Babel was probably one of these zuggurats.

Wooley found more than a thousand tombs at Ur, but 16 from the first dynasty (2700-2500 B.C.) were so impressive in architecture and contents that they are known as the "royal tombs" of Ur. The beautiful "Standard of Ur" was uncovered in one of these tombs. It is a panorama of war and peace and has many small figures made of white seashell set into a background of lapis lazuli. It shows men of Ur marching off to war with their horse-drawn battle chariots, and after their triumph, they celebrated with sacrifice and feast. The "Standard of Ur" and many other treasures that Wooley uncovered are now displayed in the British Museum's Ur Room. These treasures include a gold helmet weighing 15 carats and a golden lyre with the head of a bull.

Ziggurat at Ur of the Chaldees.

The royal tombs yielded evidence that "human sacrifice" was practiced at Ur and that when a king died, his servants accompanied him into the underworld. The fine dress and peaceful arrangement of bodies in the royal tombs indicates that the servants died willingly, probably from drinking poison. A woman was found with her fingers still on the strings of a harp, evidently playing at the king's body at the moment of her death.

The royal tombs at Ur were already several hundred years old when Abraham and Sarah lived at Ur; these tombs show that Ur had a highly advanced culture at that time.

A Brave Little Jewish Girl

The Tomb of the Patriarchs, built over the Cave of Machpelah in Hebron, is probably an authentic archaeological site. When Sarah died, Abraham purchased the Cave of Machpelah from Ephron the Hittite as a burial tomb (Genesis 23:1-23). Later, when Abraham died, Isaac and Ishmael buried him beside Sarah (Genesis 25:7-11). Two generations later when Jacob died in Egypt, his sons had him embalmed after the Egyptian custom, and the body was carried back to the Cave of Machpelah with chariots and horsemen and a great company of mourners (Genesis 50:1-14).

The massive building that now stands over the cave was built by Herod the Great during the 30 years before Jesus' birth. It is the most complete Herodian building still standing in the Bible land. When the Muslim armies conquered the Bible land in 638 A.D., they took control of the Tomb of the Patriarchs; except for the Crusader period, it has been a Muslim holy place ever since. For exactly 700 years, from 1267 A.D. until 1967, Jews were barred from entering the Tomb of the Patriarchs. Today, the Tomb is Islam's fourth holiest shrine, after Mecca, Medina, and the temple mount in Jerusalem. The

Muslims have never allowed archaeological work in the Cave of Machpelah, and as far as is known, no one had entered the cave for many centuries.

The Six Days War in 1967 changed that. The Israeli army under the command of General Moshe Dayan defeated the Arabs and captured all the West Bank, including Hebron and the Tomb of the Patriarchs. General Dayan and other Israelis were determined to explore the cave. The Tomb has a small stone opening down through the Herodian floor into the cave beneath. But the opening is only 11 inches wide, and they could not find an Israeli soldier small enough to squeeze through. So the Jews found a slender 12-year-old girl named Michal who wasn't afraid of ghosts or spirits, scorpions or snakes, and who agreed to explore the cave.

The Muslims would have been enraged had they known what was planned; so, on the night of October 9, 1968, under the cover of darkness, Michal, her father and some Israeli soldiers slipped into the Tomb of the Patriarchs. Carrying a light and camera, Michal wriggled through the 11-inch opening and was lowered by rope to the floor of the cave.

Michal found herself in a square room with three tombstones at one end. Whether they are from Crusader days, or earlier, we do not know. Otherwise, the square room contained only paper, trash and money that had been dropped down through the opening. Michal also found a narrow corridor — she stepped it off and found it 34 paces long — leading from the room. At the end of the corridor, she found a flight of 15 steps and a sealed wall.

Thanks to a very brave little Jewish girl, we have had a glimpse of what lies underneath the Tomb of the Patriarchs. But we still have no idea of what archaeologists might uncover if they were allowed to excavate there.

The Ivory Pomegranate

The Israel Museum in Jerusalem has a small ivory pomegranate on display, which archaeologists believe was used in Solomon's temple around 700 B.C. If so, the pomegranate is the only artifact from the first temple that has ever been discovered and is a priceless treasure.

The recovery of the pomegranate is shrouded in intrigue and suspense. Archaeologists first learned of the pomegranate in the *Biblical Archaeology Review* (Jan./Feb., 1984). Andre Lamaire, a scholar interested in ancient Hebrew inscriptions, reported that when he was in Jerusalem in 1979, he visited an antiquities dealer who showed him a small pomegranate, made of ivory, one-and-a-half inches high. It had an inscription in archaic Hebrew, and the shape of the letters was very similar to the inscription found in King Hezekiah's tunnel built about 700 B.C. Some of the letters were missing, but Lamaire thought that when the letters were restored, the inscription would read, "Belonging to the Temple of the Lord, holy to the priests." If so, Lamaire thought that the pomegranate was a decoration on top of a scepter carried by some priest in the temple around 700 B.C. The Israel Museum has such ivory scepters, decorated with pomegranates, that were found at Lachish and date from around 1200 B.C.

But Lamaire had to wonder, "Was the little pomegranate genuine or a fake?" He examined it carefully under a magnifying glass, found ancient patina in the incised Hebrew letters, and was convinced that the pomegranate was genuine. He was allowed to photograph the pomegranate, and wrote an article illustrated with striking pictures. It included a statement from Harvard scholar Frank Cross who said there was no doubt about the pomegranate's authenticity, and called it a "priceless" treasure.

But Lamaire reported that he had not been able to learn who owned the pomegranate or where it had been discovered. He added, "Worse, I do not know where the object is today."

The next chapter in the unfolding mystery of the pomegranate came four years later, in August, 1988, when the Associated Press reported from Jerusalem that the pomegranate had been returned to Israel and had been put on display in the Israel Museum. Apparently, the pomegranate was smuggled out of Israel illegally, for the Israel Museum had to pay $550,000 into a secret Swiss bank account to secure its return. Officials were reluctant to spend so much money to get the pomegranate back, but finally agreed to the $550,000 after months of negotiation.

Meir Meyer, vice chairman of the Israel Museum, said, "We have never had anything that was in Solomon's temple. Minuscule as it is, this is an exquisite treasure."

The Museum considers the pomegranate such a national treasure that it opened a large room with only two tiny artifacts on display in the room — the pomegranate and a little silver amulet, which will be described in chapter three.

CHAPTER TWO

The Divided Kingdom

Bill Humble:

The Old Testament is a book of history. It tells about real people like Abraham and Sarah, King Solomon, King Hezekiah and David. It tells about real places like Jerusalem and Hebron, and it tells about real events that cover 1,500 years of ancient history.

Archaeology also deals with the ancient past, and, over the last hundred years, there have been many discoveries of archaeology that have given us a picture-window into the biblical world.

Let's go back to the time of David and Solomon, 1000 B.C., for an example of this. After David captured Jerusalem, Solomon built the temple here on Mt. Moriah where the Dome of the Rock stands today. But after Solomon died about 930 B.C., the kingdom was divided, and, according to 1 Kings 14, five years later Pharaoh Shishak of Egypt invaded Judah, attacked Jerusalem, and plundered the temple.

At the temple of Karnak in Egypt, we have Shishak's own account of this same invasion, listing many of the cities of Judah he captured and plundered.

Archaeologists have also found a golden bracelet that Shishak made for his son. We wonder where the gold came from. Perhaps from the temple in Jerusalem?

The death of Solomon ushered in a tragic chapter in Old Testament history.

Solomon died about 930 B.C., and at his death the Jewish kingdom divided into two rival nations — Israel in the North and Judah in the South. Fifty years later in 880 B.C., King Omri purchased the hill of Samaria and built an enormous city here. The wall behind me is part of that original Israelite wall of the city built by Omri in 880 B.C. The city endured for 150 years until finally destroyed by the Assyrians in 721 B.C., and the people were carried away into Assyrian captivity, never to return.

When King Omri, the builder of Samaria, died in 861 B.C., he was followed on the throne by his son Ahab. And when Ahab married a Phoenician princess named Jezebel, she brought Baal worship and an extravagant palace life to Israel.

The palace of Ahab and Jezebel has been excavated and these are the ruins that lie behind me here. Ahab and Jezebel are denounced by the Old Testament prophets for their idolatry, their life of luxury, and their oppression of the poor. The prophets talk about the palaces of ivory, and when the archaeologists worked here, they discovered many pieces of ivory that once decorated this elaborate palace. These ivory pieces are now on display in the Israel Museum in Jerusalem.

One of the most beautiful pieces is a column of palm trees, seven inches high, representing the tree of life that is often seen in ancient art. A pair of lotus blossoms spring from the trunk of each tree.

Ivory carving was a specialty of Phoenician artisans, and this work may have been done in Phoenicia or by Phoenician artists that Jezebel brought to Samaria. They often used Egyptian motifs, like the child god Horus sitting on a lotus.

This piece shows a lion killing a bull. The lion's teeth are sunk in the bull's throat, and the bull is in the throes of dying.

This beautiful sphinx is a winged creature with a human head (an Egyptian head) and the body of a lion. The sphinx is striding through a thicket of lotus blossoms. Some scholars believe that the cherubim in Solomon's temple looked like this.

Two small lions are the best examples of full pieces carved in the round. They were furniture decorations and were attached with pegs in the holes.

Ivory was highly prized in the ancient world. According to 1 Kings 10:22, Solomon's fleet came in once every three years with gold and silver and ivory.

These ivories from Samaria give us a graphic picture of Ahab's luxurious palace and the "beds of ivory" denounced by Amos and Hosea.

Ten years later after Ahab's death, Jehu was the king in Israel. The Assyrians under Shalmaneser set up the Black Obelisk at Nimrud to commemorate his victories. The obelisk, now in the British Museum, shows the power of the Assyrians. One panel shows a figure prostrate before the Assyrian king, and the inscription says, "This is Jehu, son of Omri." This was an unhappy time in Jehu's reign, but this scene on the Black Obelisk is very important because it is the only contemporary picture of a Hebrew king in existence — Jehu, who reigned about 840 B.C.

Ivory pomegranate from priest's scepter. Only artifact from first temple ever discovered. Courtesy Israel Museum, Jerusalem.

After Ahab and Jehu the Assyrian threat grew, and a dark shadow from the East hung over the city of Samaria. Samaria was destroyed by the Assyrians in 721 B.C., and many of the people were carried away into Assyrian captivity, never to return. But the Assyrians sent in colonists to resettle the land, and evidently there was intermarriage between the Assyrian colonists and the Israelites who remained behind, and the result was the Samaritan people.

They still endure as a distinct race, and at Nablus, we meet Saloom, one of the Samaritan priests.

Saloom:

Old Samaritans, they live in Nablus. The number for Samaritans is about 570; 300 they live in Nablus here; 270 they live in Israel. And we are two families, priest family and Samaritan family. The priest family, like us here, this family don't work, only serve in synagogue; and this family don't shave and don't cut hair. This family from Levi, the son of Jacob. The Samaritan family is from the two sons of Joseph, Ephraim and Manasseh. The priest family only serve in synagogue. The Samaritans believe that the holy mountain is Gerezim here. And this city is between two mountains, here Gerezim and here Ebal, here blessing mountain and here cursing mountain. The city, they call it Nablus, a Greek name for 1,700 years. The real name for this city in the Bible is Shechem.

Bill Humble:

The Samaritans have an ancient manuscript of the Pentateuch, written on sheep skin, which they bring out for us to see. Scholars believe that this manuscript is about 1,500 years old and a valuable witness to the Old Testament.

The Samaritans still keep the three feasts of the Old Testament.

Saloom:

We have three feasts, the first the feast of Passover sacrifice. This feast must be in April. At the month of April all Samaritans go up to the top of Mount Gerezim and stay at the top of the mountain for seven days to make the sacrifice. At the first day till now, we bring 25 sheep or 27 lambs, and we make a sacrifice for God. And we eat at this feast a white bread we call it *matsa.* This feast is to remember when Israel left Egypt with guide Moses. The second feast, the feast of Pentecost, the 50 days after passover, seven weeks, is to remember when God gave Moses the Ten Commandments.

Bill Humble:

Animal sacrifices on the Passover — just like the days of Moses and Aaron more than 3,000 years ago.

Four hundred years after Samaria was destroyed by the Assyrians, Alexander the Great and his armies came through the Bible land, and with their rebuilding, Samaria became a Greek city.

This circular tower was part of Alexander the Great's building. Notice the stone work. It is much more skilled than the walls of Omri's city that were built 500 years earlier.

Samaria was rebuilt a second time by Herod the Great about 20 years before Jesus' birth. This is the Roman forum from Herod's city.

After the fall of Samaria in 721 B.C., the Assyrian armies moved south into Judah.

Lachish is another very important archaeological site from Old Testament times. This was a Canaanite city for 2,000 years before it was destroyed by Joshua.

It was rebuilt and fortified by Rehoboam, then by the later kings of Judah, and in 701 B.C. it was besieged and destroyed by Sennacherib, King of Assyria. At the time it was the second largest city in Judah.

Lachish had been a major Canaanite city as early as 3000 B.C., and the reason was its strategic location.

Joseph Shulam:

Lachish is located geographically here on the main road that led between Jerusalem and Egypt, and, of course, this is the road that in the New Testament one reads about the Ethiopian eunuch taking from Jerusalem through Gaza on down to Egypt and Ethiopia. It is a very important site archaeologically because it has been dug for a long period of time since the beginning of our century.

Bill Humble:

The archaeologists cut a deep trench through the tell and this made it possible to identify 13 different cities built on top of one another.

Joseph Shulam:

Here at Lachish the levels of civilization stretch from 2800 B.C. when the city was in its peak during the Canaanite period, in the Middle Bronze period, all the way to Sennacherib and Nebuchadnezzar.

Bill Humble:

Notice how the different levels of civilization are marked on the walls of the trench. According to Joshua 10, it only took Joshua and his men two days to capture Lachish. Level nine marks that Canaanite city that Joshua destroyed and burned. You can still see the layer of gray ashes.

Lachish lay in ruins for 200 years; then it was rebuilt and fortified by King Rehoboam, and later kings of Judah continued the building. The most impressive ruin left by the Judaean kings is a large platform where their fortress stood.

Survivors of Lachish going into captivity. Stone relief from Sennacherib's palace at Nineveh.

The wall that we have behind me is the platform of that citadel or fortress. It was first rebuilt by Rehoboam; then nearly all the kings of Judah after Rehoboam continued to rebuild the fortress and the palace on this citadel.

This platform is 250 feet long and 100 feet wide, and it served as the foundation for several great buildings, but none of the buildings have survived.

Archaeologists are now working in Lachish. They have uncovered the large city gate on the west side of the tell. The gate has three chambers and is the largest found anywhere in Israel. In these excavations at the gate they have found large catapult stones. These may have been hurled at the gate in the Assyrian siege.

Just south of the gate, archaeologists have identified this debris as the siege ramp that the Assyrians built to mount their attack against the city wall.

Lachish was besieged and destroyed by Assyrian armies under Sennacherib in 701 B.C. At the time Lachish was the second most important city in Judah, and its loss was very important to King Hezekiah. Archaeologically, Lachish is very important to us because there is no other event of ancient history for which we have so many different kinds of records as we have here. We have the Bible account in 2 Chronicles 32:1-23. We have the Assyrian records. We have the archaeological ruins here at the site. And we have a great mural done in stone by Sennacherib.

Sennacherib must have thought that the conquest of Lachish was his finest hour. For he built a great new palace at Nineveh — he called it the "palace without a rival" — and the architectural focus of that palace was a room decorated with reliefs, carved in stone, picturing his siege of Lachish. These reliefs were discovered in the 1850s and are now in the British Museum with a copy in the Israel Museum.

The relief shows a strong Assyrian army with archers and spearmen attacking the walls of Lachish. They have built a ramp and are marching up the ramp to attack the city gate. The heaviest fighting is around the gate. There are many Israelite defenders on the gate.

The Assyrians are trying to break down the gate with a battering ram. The defenders above throw burning torches down on the Assyrian war machine, and a soldier on the battering ram uses a long-handled bucket to pour water on the torches. After the city falls, the Assyrians carry away booty and treasure.

The Assyrians take some prisoners, and some of them kneel before Sennacherib and beg for their lives. Others are tortured, stretched out naked and flayed alive. Some are impaled on sharpened stakes — a cruel form of execution.

After Lachish has fallen, the people face a long thousand-mile journey into Assyrian exile. Many are starting the journey on foot. Here's an oxcart with two frightened children riding on it. And here, two little boys cling to their father.

Sennacherib sits on his throne watching the human tragedy. Notice that his head has been defaced — and this is not usual in ancient art. There's an inscription over his throne: "I am Sennacherib . . . sitting on my throne at Lachish." This is remarkable art, carved in stone 2,700 years ago, and all the more remarkable because it pictures the siege of Lachish that the Bible records.

After Lachish had fallen, Sennacherib and his armies laid siege to Jerusalem. But according to the Bible, the prophet Isaiah encouraged King Hezekiah to hold out, and he did, and Jerusalem was spared. The British Museum has a clay prism of Sennacherib giving his account of the invasion. He only says that he shut up Hezekiah in his royal city "like a bird in a cage." So, according to this Assyrian record, Jerusalem was spared just like the Bible says.

One thing that saved Jerusalem from Assyrian destruction was a tunnel that Hezekiah built to bring water into the city. This tunnel was discovered in 1880, and it's possible to wade through it today.

The tunnel is one-third of a mile long, cut through the solid rock. It brings water from the Gihon Spring, outside the city wall, to the Pool of Siloam. The Gihon Spring had been Jerusalem's water supply from time immemorial.

When you walk through this tunnel, you are hiking back in history 2,700 years to the time when Jerusalem was threatened with Assyrian siege. Hezekiah built the tunnel to provide a water supply for the city of Jerusalem. Without a water supply the city would have been destroyed by the Assyrians, and Hezekiah built this tunnel to make sure there would be a water supply for the city. You can read about it in 2 Kings 20.

Near the south end of the tunnel, they found an inscription in the wall, in archaic Hebrew, from the days of Hezekiah. It is a vivid description of the day the tunnel was finished — how the two crews, working from either end, cut through the last three cubits of rock and saw the water begin flowing through the tunnel.

We come out of the tunnel at the Pool of Siloam. This is where Jesus healed the blind man in John 9.

When we visit historic places like Hezekiah's tunnel, the Pool of Siloam, and Lachish, the Bible springs to life and becomes a living book.

Joseph Shulam:

I have been living in this land for 40 years of my life, and I have traveled it up and down, its hills and valleys, many many times. I have been studying archaeology and the Bible for 25 years, and in spite of this fact, every time I come to these sites, it brings back to mind and memory that, as Bible-believing people, we don't deal with myth. We are dealing with reality.

Bill Humble:

Over the last hundred years, a vast amount of archaeological work has been done here in the Bible land, and year after year discoveries have been made that illuminate the Bible and sometimes confirm the historical accuracy of the Bible.

I once had a chance to study under William F. Albright, then the world's foremost archaeologist. And to use Dr. Albright's exact words: "Thanks to the discoveries of archaeology, we know that the Bible's historical memory is incredibly accurate."

Scriptures for Study

1 Kings 16:21-28. Omri builds Samaria.
1 Kings 16-22. Ahab, Jezebel and Elijah.
2 Kings 17:1-23. Fall of Samaria.
2 Kings 17:24-28. Origin of Samaritans.
2 Kings 18-19. Assyrian siege of Jerusalem.
2 Kings 20:20,21; 2 Chronicles 32:1-8. Hezekiah's tunnel.

Notes from Archaeology

Excavations at Samaria

Ancient Samaria is one of the most impressive archaeological sites anywhere in Israel. It is dimpressive because of its location on a hilltop, 300 feet above the surrounding valleys, 42 miles north of Jerusalem. King Omri purchased this hill from Shemer for two talents of silver and built a new city, Samaria, on the hilltop about 880 B.C. (2 Kings 16:24). The city was in a strategic location to command trade routes northward to the Valley of Jezreel, and it served as the capital of the northern kingdom until its destruction. The kings of Israel could see the Mediterranean Sea, 25 miles to the west, from their royal citadel.

Samaria is also impressive because so many different levels of civilization have been uncovered in the excavations, levels so distinctive that they can be identified even by untrained observers.

The first excavations at Samaria were done by a Harvard team under the direction of Reisner and Fisher (1908-1910). Later excavations (1931-1935), directed by J.W. Crowfoot with the help of Kathleen Kenyon, were much more extensive and were supported by Harvard, the Hebrew University in Jerusalem, and the Palestine Exploration Fund.

The archaeologists have found walls and the remains of buildings that were built by Omri and his son Ahab in the ninth century B.C. They have found the royal palace where Ahab and his Phoenician Queen Jezebel lived. The palace measured about 80 by 90 feet and was probably two stories high. Near the palace they found a large, shallow pool, which may be the "pool of Samaria" where Ahab's blood was washed out of his chariot after his death at Ramoth-Gilead (1 Kings 22:38).

Today, visitors to the Israel Museum in Jerusalem are captivated by the beauty of ivory carvings that archaeologists found in the palace of Ahab and Jezebel. There are more than 500 fragments of carved ivory that once decorated the walls and furniture in Ahab's palace. The work was probably done by Phoenician artisans, but many of their decorative motifs are Egyptian. The ivory carvings show that the Old Testament denunciations of "beds of ivory" (Amos 6:4; 1 Kings 22:39) were not exaggerated.

Another important discovery was the "Samaria ostraca" — 63 pieces of broken pottery with inscriptions from the time of King Jereboam II (770 B.C.). The ostraca are receipts and tax records for oil, wine and barley. They are important because few other examples of Hebrew writing survive from such an early date. Also, because of the frequent use of "Baal" in proper names, the ostraca show that Baal worship was widespread in Israel at the time.

Samaria was destroyed in 721 B.C. by the Assyrian king Sargon II after a three-year siege, and, according to Sargon's records, he carried 27,290 Israelites into Assyrian captivity. (According to 2 Kings 17:1-6, the siege began under Shalmaneser, Sargon's father, but Sargon had probably succeeded to the throne by the time the city fell.) People from other conquered lands were resettled in Samaria, and the city of Samaria was rebuilt, "better than it was before its destruction," if we trust Sargon's claims.

Four hundred years later, when Alexander the Great's armies occupied the Bible land, Samaria was transformed into a Hellenistic (Greek) city. Alexander strengthened the city's fortifications. Massive circular towers, each more than 40 feet in diameter, are still standing from the days of Alexander the Great. These towers have been called "the finest monuments of the Hellenistic age" to be seen anywhere in Israel today.

Herod the Great did vast building at Samaria during the 30 years before Jesus' birth. Herod built a large Roman-style forum and many new buildings, including a temple to the emperor Augustus. The temple was located on the summit of the acropolis, and the broad steps leading up to the temple are still to be seen. Herod also built a new defensive wall, two miles long, around the city with strong towers at strategic locations in the wall. A number of key events in Herod the Great's life happened at Samaria. He married Mariamne at Samaria. Mariamne was the Maccabean princess whom he loved madly but later executed. Herod had two sons by Mariamne. He favored these sons and sent them to Rome for the finest possible education, but later had them executed at Samaria.

When Herod rebuilt Samaria, he renamed it Sebaste (the Greek word for Augustus) to honor the emperor. The name persists today in a little Arab village, Sebastiyeh, located on the ancient site.

The Samaritans

The Samaritans appear in the New Testament in Jesus' parable of the Good Samaritan, in His conversation with the Samaritan woman at Jacob's well, and in other passages. The descendants of those ancient Samaritans still live in the Bible land, and though they have dwindled to a small community of less than 1,000, they have managed to maintain their identity as a distinct people for well over 2,000 years.

It is not clear just how the Samaritan people originated. We know that Samaria was destroyed by the Assyrians in 721 B.C. and that the people of the northern kingdom, some of them at least, were carried away into Assyrian captivity (2 Kings 17:1-6). We also know that Assyria sent in colonists from the East "and placed them in the cities of Samaria instead of the people of Israel." We also know that these settlers did not fear the Lord, and when they were attacked by lions, the Assyrian king sent a Jewish priest back to Samaria to teach them about "the god of the land" (2 Kings 17:24-28). But the biblical record does *not* say that there was intermarriage between the Jews of the land and the Assyrian colonists, though this is often assumed.

Today, the Samaritans believe that they are true Jews, direct descendants of northern kingdom Jews who were not carried into captivity. They also believe that their alienation from other Jews began when Eli set up the sanctuary in Shiloh, whereas the true sanctuary of God was always Mt. Gerezim. The Jews, on the other hand, see the Samaritans as descendants of the Assyrian settlers in the land, and they regard Samaritans as little better than Gentiles.

The truth probably lies somewhere between these two extreme views, and, if so, the familiar story of intermarriage between the northern kingdom Jews who were not exiles and the Assyrian settlers may well be true.

After the Jews returned from Babylonian exile in 536 B.C. and rebuilt their temple in Jerusalem, the Samaritans built a rival temple on Mt. Gerezim. This Samaritan temple was destroyed by John Hyrcanus during the Maccabean age in 128 B.C. The Samaritans probably continued to worship on Mt. Gerezim after their temple had been destroyed, for as the Samaritan woman at Jacob's well reminded Jesus, "Our fathers worshiped God on this mountain" (John 4:20). During the Jews' Bar Kochba revolt in 132 A.D., the Samaritans supported Rome, and the grateful Emperor Hadrian allowed them to rebuild their temple. But this second Samaritan temple was later destroyed.

There were communities of Samaritans in many cities, including Cairo, during the middle ages, but these communities disappeared long ago. Today there are less than 1,000 Samaritans. They live in Nablus at the base of Mt. Gerezim, and in Joppa. With such a small population and centuries of marriage within the community, Samaritans have genetic problems.

But they now allow their people to marry outside the community if the one they marry will embrace the Samaritan faith.

The Samaritans believe in God and Moses, but they accept only the Torah, the five books of Moses, as Scripture. They believe that Mt. Gerezim is the true sanctuary of God, and even though they no longer have a temple on Gerezim, they still observe the Passover with animal sacrifices as in the days of Moses. They also celebrate Pentecost and the Feast of Booths with pilgrimages to the summit of Gerezim.

Hezekiah Tunnel Inscription

In 1880 an inscription was discovered in the wall of the Hezekiah tunnel near the south end where it enters the Pool of Siloam. The inscription stone is nearly two feet wide and gives a vivid description of how workmen, cutting from either end, met and completed the tunnel. The inscription is in archaic Hebrew and confirms that the present tunnel is the one that King Hezekiah built about 701 B.C. to protect Jerusalem's water supply from the Assyrian army.

The inscription stone was later removed from the wall of the tunnel and is now displayed in the Istanbul Museum. The inscription says:

> "This is the story of the boring through. While the workmen lifted the pick each toward his fellow and while three cubits remained to be bored through, the voice of a man was heard calling to his fellow, for there was a split in the rock on the right hand and on the left. And on the day of the boring through, the tunnellers struck, each in the direction of his fellows, pick against pick. And the water started to flow from the source to the pool, 1,200 cubits. And the height of the rock above the heads of the tunnellers was 100 cubits."

Chapter Three

The Dead Sea Scrolls

Bill Humble:

Some of the most exciting discoveries of archaeology are written records, such as inscriptions on stone, inscriptions on coins, manuscripts, even manuscripts of the Bible. The Dead Sea Scrolls are an example of this because no archaeological discovery of the 20th century has been more exciting than the scrolls.

The Dead Sea Scrolls were discovered in 1947 here at Qumran overlooking the north end of the Dead Sea. The first scrolls were found by accident by a shepherd boy of the Taamirah Bedouin tribe. Elias Subeh of Bethlehem belongs to that tribe, and his father was the sheik of the tribe at the time. Elias recalls how it happened.

Elias Subeh:

But after that shepherd lost a goat here, he went up to that cave up the hill ahead of us and saw cylindric jars. He went in and thought it could be gold in the jars. He opened the first one — scrolls. The second — another scroll. Destroying the jars, he picked up the scrolls, and about four weeks later, the shepherd brought to my father to Bethlehem three scrolls. He brought Isaiah, the Book of Discipline, and Habakkuk. He think I could sell them, and I used to carry Isaiah 24-feet long scroll in my car. I show it to many people. They tell me, "It is witchcraft; get rid of it." And my father is the one who told the shepherd to take the scrolls to a shoemaker in Bethlehem by the name of Kando.

Bill Humble:

The cave where the shepherd found the scrolls was here on a desert hillside about eight miles south of Jericho. And hidden in the cave, protected in pottery jars, he found seven old manuscripts written on leather.

One of them, which you see here, would prove to be a 2,000-year-old manuscript of Isaiah — the oldest manuscript of a complete book of the Bible ever discovered.

Kando, the shoemaker, paid the shepherd $25 for the old leather manuscripts. Thankfully, he didn't use them to repair shoes, but instead, he sold four of them to the bishop of his Syrian Orthodox Church in Jerusalem. The Isaiah scroll was photographed, and when William F. Albright, the famous American archaeologist, saw the pictures, he called it the greatest manuscript discovery of modern times. And the Syrian bishop knew he had a good buy in the scrolls.

Elias Subeh:

The bishop took them over to the U.S.A. and sold them for $275,000 to a man named Samuel Gottesman. So you can imagine, the poor shepherd brought to light the biggest discovery of the 20th century, and what he got out of the whole deal was $25. And that's why since 1947 when he see me in Bethlehem, he turn his back to me. He thinks I am crazy when I told him they were witchcraft; those scrolls were.

Bill Humble:

After the seven manuscripts were discovered in that first cave in 1947, the Bedouin shepherds and archaeologists spent the next ten years exploring hundreds and hundreds of caves in these mountainsides looking for additional scrolls. And in 10 caves they found manuscripts or at least fragments of what had once been manuscripts. The most important was Cave 4, that we see here, that was found in 1952.

Cave 4 did not have any complete manuscripts like Cave 1, but it had thousands of fragments of manuscripts. There were no jars in Cave 4 to protect the scrolls, so lying on the ground for nearly 2,000 years, they had fallen to pieces.

After years of study, scholars identified nearly 400 different manuscripts from Cave 4. Almost a hundred of these were biblical manuscripts including every book of the Old Testament except Esther.

As the Bedouin shepherds and archaeologists combed the mountainsides looking for more caves, the Bedouin made most of the discoveries. They knew the land.

The Jordanian Department of Antiquities authorized Kando to buy the scrolls from the Bedouin, and Kando became a famous antiquities dealer with a shop in Jerusalem.

As the shepherds found more caves — six in the summer of 1955 — they also found a way to increase their income.

Elias Subeh:

I have seen the shepherds cutting the scrolls to

inches, selling inch by inch because they think they could get more money.

Bill Humble:

When archaeologists learned of the first seven scrolls, they had many questions.

Where was the cave where the scrolls were found?

Who had copied them?

Why were they hidden in the cave?

They soon realized that an ancient ruin near the cave — Khirbet Qumran — might have the answers. Two archaeologists, Lancaster Harding and Roland DeVaux, began excavating Qumran in 1953 and worked at the site for four years. Their discoveries, along with the Manual of Discipline, one of the scrolls from Cave 1, have answered most of the questions.

They learned that Qumran was a Jewish monastic community, probably Essenes. They settled here in the Judean desert about 130 B.C., and except for 30 years during Herod the Great's reign, they lived here for 200 years 'til they were destroyed by the Romans.

The Essenes believed that the Jewish nation had fallen away from God. They were the faithful remnant, "sons of light," and they had fled to the wilderness to wait for the end of days and the kingdom. They were looking for two messiahs — a priest and ruler like David.

These ruins where they lived tell us a lot about the Essene community. This was the only section of the community that was two stories high. It was a tall tower, probably intended for the protection of the community in time of attack.

The archaeologists found the scriptorium, or library, where the Essenes worked on the scrolls. Ink pots were even found here, along with stone tables and benches. They also found a piece of pottery with the Hebrew alphabet crudely lettered on it, maybe the work of some young scribe just beginning his training.

Hills overlooking Dead Sea with Qumran ruins in foreground.

We know from the Manual of Discipline, one of the manuscripts found in Cave 1, that the Essenes worked in shifts 24 hours a day in this library, or scriptorium, writing commentaries and copying their precious manuscripts of the Bible.

The largest room in the building, 75 feet long, has been called the Hall of the Congregation. We know from the manual of Discipline that the men of the congregation met here for all their meals together, and every meal was a sort of sacred meal. As the men of the congregation ate together, one of them would be reading from the Scripture or expounding the Scripture. So there was a sacred import to each one of their meals.

Qumran also had an elaborate water system with large cisterns and a water channel running through the buildings. Here's a floor plan of the buildings. The scriptorium is No. 2 and the water system is shown in blue. The Essenes had to have a water supply because it was so hot in the desert.

Elias Subeh:

I feel sorry for those Essenes spending over 150 years here in this climate, and in that time there was no air-conditioning. And this will prove when the British were here — instead of saying, "Go to hell," they used to say, "Go to Jericho." It's about 100 now, but in July and August it gets to 135 or 140 here.

Bill Humble:

Also, the Essenes practiced ceremonial immersion — baptism — and they had to have running water in their *mikvoth,* or baptistries.

What about food? There are fresh water springs down near the Dead Sea, and the Essenes probably raised enough grain down there to feed the community. And those springs probably explain why the Essenes settled here in the first place.

Living here in solitude, the Essenes were waiting for God's kingdom to come. But their solitude was shattered in 68 A.D. when the Jews rebelled against Rome. The Roman army marched down the Jordan valley and destroyed Jericho, then Qumran. As the army approached, the Essenes must have hidden their manuscripts in the caves. The men may have perished, but their scrolls survived, to be discovered by accident in 1947.

The seven scrolls from Cave 1 are on display in the Shrine of the Book in Jerusalem, built in honor of Samuel Gottesman who bought the scrolls from the Syrian bishop and returned them to Israel.

The outside of the museum looks like the lid of one of the pottery jars from Cave 1. Inside, two of the jars the shepherd found are on display. One is about 3 feet tall. The second is a little shorter.

The inside of the museum is like a cave and is rather dark, to give the illusion of being in a cave and to protect the scrolls from light.

The Isaiah scroll is the museum's treasure, and it is displayed in a circular case in the center of the room. This scroll is 2,000 years old, and this makes it the oldest manuscript of a complete book of the Bible that has ever been discovered. It has every chapter and every verse that we have in our Bibles. Except for a few very minor variations, the Hebrew text is identical with the Massoretic text that was used for all our English translations of the Bible.

Some scholars believe there were two Isaiahs with a break in the book between chapters 39 and 40. But the Isaiah scroll has no such break — only a little mark to show the end of chapter 39 and the beginning of chapter 40.

Another scroll from Cave 1 is this commentary on Habakkuk. In their commentary the Essenes applied everything in Habakkuk to their own times.

Another scroll is the War of the Sons of Light and the Sons of Darkness. It describes the warfare between good and evil, and some of the language, like "sons of light," sounds like the gospel of John.

Except for Isaiah, the Manual of Discipline is the most valuable scroll because it has all the rules and regulations that governed the Qumran community. It tells how people joined the community, how they held everything in common, and it gives the rules of conduct they lived under.

The Temple Scroll is the longest of the Dead Sea Scrolls, longer than Isaiah, and it remained hidden until 1967.

Elias Subeh:

I have just mentioned that the shepherds found many scrolls after the discovery of May '47. One of the discoveries the shepherds found later was the Temple Scroll which they took to Bethlehem, and Kando bought it. I don't know how much he paid for it. And it was in his home hidden in the ground. When the '67 war took over, Dayan and Yadin came to Bethlehem and told Mr. Kando, "We know you have a scroll." Kando took it out of the ground, and Dayan and Yadin bought it for $70,000.

Bill Humble:

After Yigael Yadin sent army officers to Bethlehem to recover the scroll, he spent several years studying it and then published it. The Temple Scroll proved to be an Essene document that deals with the temple, the statutes of the king, and the Old Testament feasts.

The Shrine of the Book also has some letters from the Second Jewish Revolt in 132 A.D., and they are displayed in this tunnel-like room. These letters were found in 1961 in a cave several miles north of Qumran. They were written on papyrus by Simon Bar Kochba, who led the Second Revolt.

Bar Kochba wrote this letter to his commanders at Ein Gedi.

In this letter Bar Kochba mentions one of his generals, *Yeshua,* the first word on the second line. *Yeshua* is the exact name, in Hebrew, of Jesus, and this shows how the name Jesus was written in the first century.

In this letter Bar Kochba orders one of his generals to put the Galileans in fetters. The "Galileans" were the Jewish Christians, and this is the first tangible evidence outside the New Testament of the persecution of believers.

Now let's talk about the value of the scrolls found at Qumran. Why have they been called the most important manuscript discovery of the 20th century?

Before the scrolls were discovered, the oldest Hebrew manuscript of the Old Testament was the Aleppo Codex, also on display at the Shrine of the Book. It was copied about 900 A.D. This means that the Isaiah scroll is a thousand years older than the oldest Hebrew manuscript before its discovery. And this means that in the Dead Sea Scrolls scholars now have invaluable new sources for studying the text of the Old Testament.

The scrolls are also valuable because of the information they have about community life at Qumran.

Joseph Shulam:

The community at Qumran and the New Testament community had many similarities. For example, when one reads the book of Acts and finds the believers putting all things in common, the model for such a community obviously was Qumran, that had already been living this way for over a hundred years in the vicinity of Jerusalem.

Bill Humble:

Remember that the Essenes had a water system at Qumran that provided running water for their baptisms.

Joseph Shulam:

The Qumran community was very conscious of the Old Testament purity laws, and for this reason they practiced ritual immersion, which we call baptism, many times a day. They practiced it every time they got ceremonially unclean.

Bill Humble:

As important as the Dead Sea Scrolls are, let's remember that there are hundreds of other ancient manuscripts of the Bible in the museums of the world.

One of the greatest is the Sinaitic manuscript in the British Museum. It was discovered at St. Catherine's Monastery by Count Tischendorf in the 1840s. This manuscript has all 27 books of the New Testament, and it was copied in the fourth century.

The oldest New Testament manuscript is the John Rylands papyrus. It's only a small part of John 18, but this manuscript was made in the first half of the second century — perhaps within 50 years of the original writing of John.

The Samaritans who live at the base of Mt. Gerezim have an ancient manuscript of the Pentateuch. One of their priests, Saloom, shows it to us.

Saloom:

Twenty-five meters long, and about 100 feet, this is only the five books of Moses, the Pentateuch, Genesis — Exodus, Leviticus, Numbers, Deuteronomy. This book was written on the skin of the sacrifices, the skin of the sheep of the sacrifice. Who wrote it? The fourth generation from Aaron.

Bill Humble:

Scholars believe that this manuscript is about 1,500

years old, and it's another valuable witness to the text of the Old Testament.

In 1980 archaeologists found a burial cave in Jerusalem, 2,700 years old and never disturbed. This silver amulet was in the cave, and when it was unrolled, it proved to be the priestly blessing in Numbers 6, engraved in the silver:

"The Lord bless you and keep you,
The Lord make his face to shine upon you,
and give you peace."

This is now the oldest fragment of Scripture ever discovered, about 500 years older that the Dead Sea Scrolls.

Thanks to the Dead Sea Scrolls and these many other manuscripts, we can have great confidence in the text of the Bible. When we read the Bible, we don't need to ask, "Is this book just like it was written by Matthew and John and Paul?" We don't need to ask that question. We can be sure that it is.

Scriptures for Study

Luke 1:1-80. Birth of John the Baptist.
Matthew 3:1-13. John's ministry.
Acts 4:32-37. Community of goods in Jerusalem church.

The New Testament never mentions Qumran or the Essenes. However, some scholars think that John the Baptist might have been influenced by the Essenes. There are similarities in life style and in the locale of his ministry. Also, there are similarities between Qumran and the Jerusalem church in their holding all things in common.

Notes from Archaeology

Community Life at Qumran

The Manual of Discipline, one of the manuscripts found in Cave 1 in 1947, and the extensive excavations that were done at Qumran (1952-1956) have provided a wealth of information about community life at Qumran. Additional information comes from three ancient historians who wrote about the Essenes: Josephus, Pliny and Philo. Based on all this data, scholars now believe that Qumran was an Essene community or at least very similar to the Essenes (even though the scrolls never say explicitly that the people at Qumran were Essenes).

The cultural influences that led to the rise of Essenes and Pharisees go back to the fifth century B.C. when Greek influences began to be felt in the Bible land. Then came Alexander the Great, the Ptolemies, and the Seleucids, and it seemed to many pious Jews that a pagan, Hellenistic culture threatened their way of life. During the Maccabean period (163-63 B.C.) the Hasideans arose as a party opposing these Greek influences, and the Hasideans evolved into the Pharisees of the New Testament times and the Orthodox Jews of modern times. Another group, the Essenes, went even further than the Hasideans. Despairing and convinced that Israel was forsaking God, the Essenes retreated into the Judean desert and to other remote locations, to try to maintain their spiritual purity.

According to the Dead Sea Scrolls, the men at Qumran referred to themselves as the saints of the Most High, the faithful remnant, the sons of light, a holy people, and the community of Israel and Aaron. The group settled at Qumran in the days of John Hyrcanus (134-104 B.C.) when their "Teacher of

Righteousness" was persecuted by a "wicked priest." Even though the men at Qumran honored the "Teacher of Righteousness" and followed His teachings, they did not regard Him as the Messiah. Instead, they were looking for two messiahs to come — one a faithful priest, and the other a ruler like David.

Qumran was organized as a monastic community with priests and laity. It was not easy to join the community. When someone applied for membership, he was first examined by an overseer, an office somewhat analogous to the New Testament elder, and then by "the many." If accepted, it was for a year's probationary period, and at the end of the year the candidate might be admitted to full membership. At that point he surrendered all his property to the community, for the group held all property in common.

Were women admitted to the community? The evidence is ambiguous. The scrolls found at Qumran seem to imply that it was a male community, but female skeletons were found in the group's cemetery. The ancient historians who write of the Essenes, such as Josephus and Philo, indicate that most Essenes practiced celibacy, although some were married. Perhaps there were differences among the Essene groups on this point.

The Essenes at Qumran practiced two important religious rites: washings and ceremonial meals. There are obvious similarities with baptism and the Lord's Supper in the early church, but there were also great differences. Ceremonial baptisms were a common practice in first-century Judaism. Herod the Great's palaces had *mikvoth,* or baptistries. But these Jewish baptisms were never once-and-for-all admission into the community. Rather, they were practiced repeatedly whenever one became ceremonially unclean.

And there were many things that made one unclean, such as "going to the bathroom." Also, while the Essenes' ceremonial meals included bread and wine, there was no idea of fellowship with a Messiah who had already come and died.

Scriptorium with Dead Sea in distance.

The Old Testament scriptures were very important to the men of Qumran, and their community life focused on copying and studying the Scriptures. The Manual of Discipline shows that scribes worked on their manuscripts in shifts, 24 hours a day. The work was done in a library or scriptorium. The archaeologists found this room with tables and benches, and even ink pots. Judging from the manuscripts in the caves, Deuteronomy, Isaiah and the Psalms were the

Essenes' three favorite books. Cave 1 had two manuscripts of Isaiah. One is complete, 2,000 years old, and this makes it the oldest complete manuscript of a biblical book ever discovered. Cave 4 had fragments of at least 12 different manuscripts of Isaiah. Similarly, Cave 4 yielded fragments of at least 14 manuscripts of Deuteronomy and 10 of the Psalms.

Although the Essenes had withdrawn to the wilderness to be a holy people of God, they could not escape the Jewish-Roman war that broke out in 68 A.D. The community perished at the hands of the Roman legions. But their manuscripts, hidden in caves as the Romans approached, survived to become one of the greatest archaeological discoveries.

The Temple Scroll

The intriguing tale of the Temple Scroll began in the early 1960s. At that time, before the Six Days War of June 1967, the entire West Bank, including Bethlehem, was part of the country of Jordan. In 1960 Yigael Yadin, a prominent Israeli archaeologist who would later become Deputy Prime Minister of Israel, learned of the existence of another Dead Sea Scroll from Qumran. It was in the hands of a Bethlehem antiquities dealer named Kando, who was well known from his previous dealings in scrolls from Qumran, and it was for sale. Yadin began secret negotiations to buy the scroll, which continued for two years. At one point Yadin made a "down payment" of $10,000, but even so, the negotiations came to naught. When the Six Days War broke out in 1967, the Israeli armies won an unbelievable lightning-fast victory over their Arab enemies, and Bethlehem fell under Israeli control. Yigael Yadin was then serving as military advisor to Prime Minister Levi Eshkol.

He informed the Prime Minister about the scroll, and with his blessing Yadin sent an army officer to Bethlehem to demand the scroll. Kando removed a tile from the floor of his home, and there, hidden in a shoe box, was the scroll. Yadin later paid Kando $105,000 for the confiscated scroll (this figure is from an article in *Biblical Archaeology Review*, Sept./Oct. 1984).

Experts had to work carefully to unroll the scroll. It was written on thin animal skin, the thinnest Yadin had ever seen — about 1/250th of an inch thick. They slowly unrolled the scroll by subjecting it to high humidity to soften the 1,900-year-old leather and unrolling it a little at a time. It proved to be 27 feet long, five feet longer than the famous Isaiah scroll, making it the longest of all the Dead Sea Scrolls.

Yadin spent years studying the scroll, preparing it for publication. It proved to be an Essene document, and because half of the scroll was devoted to the temple, Yadin named it the Temple Scroll. It was copied about 50 A.D., but based on fragments of the same manuscript found in Qumran Cave 4, Yadin estimates that the original composition of the Temple Scroll was around 150 B.C. Yadin's study of the Temple Scroll convinced him that the Essenes regarded the book as *torah*, or law, which they included in their Old Testament canon.

About one-half of the Temple Scroll deals with plans for building the temple and the sacrifices that would be offered in the temple. According to 1 Chronicles 28:11-19, David gave Solomon plans for the temple, which he had received from the hands of the Lord, but the Old Testament does not include these plans. Later scribes believed that a scroll containing these plans had once existed. Yadin does not claim that the Temple Scroll is that ancient scroll, but he does believe that the Essene authors of the Temple Scroll knew that such a scroll had once existed.

Similarly, 1 Samuel 10:25 refers to an ancient book which contained the rights and duties of the kings. According to Yadin, the Essene scribe may have believed that he was preserving the contents of that missing book about the king. The Temple Scroll has laws about the marriage of the king, mobilization for war, booty taken in war, and an advisory council for the king.

The Temple Scroll also deals at length with the Jews' religious festivals, including some that are not mentioned in the Old Testament, such as "new wine" and "new oil" festivals.

The author of the Temple Scroll had an expert knowledge of the Pentateuch and stressed the strict observance of its laws. According to Yadin, the Essenes' strictness in keeping the law is perhaps the most important characteristic of the Temple Scroll. As an example, the Essenes believed that Old Testament laws dealing with ritual cleanliness in the Israelite camp in the wilderness (Deuteronomy 23:10-14, for example) had to be applied to the entire city of Jerusalem. The Essenes were forbidden to have toilets inside the city. They had to go outside the camp (city) to go to the toilet. And because that was more than a Sabbath day's journey, they just could not go on the Sabbath.

Jesus had strong condemnation for such legalism, and although the Essenes are not explicitly named in the New Testament, Jesus' teachings may have been directed against them along with the Pharisees. In the Sermon on the Mount, Jesus said, "You have heard that it was said . . . hate your enemies." Such a command is not found in the Old Testament. But in the Manual of Discipline, when a member was accepted into the Qumran community, he had to swear to love the sons of light and "hate the sons of darkness for all eternity." Jesus may have had this Essene practice in mind when he commanded his disciples, "Love your enemies."

The Silver Amulet

In 1980 archaeologists working on the shoulder of the Hinnom Valley in Jerusalem discovered an ancient burial cave. The Greek word for Hinnom is *Gehenna,* usually translated "hell," so these archaeologists were working in the Valley of Hell when they came upon this cave. The burial cave, or tomb, goes back to the seventh century B.C., not long after the days of Isaiah, Hezekiah and the Hezekiah tunnel.

Excavations showed that the burial cave had not been disturbed in 2,700 years, so its original contents were still there. The archaeologists found the bones of the dead who had been buried in the cave along with many pieces of pottery. They also found jewelry, including beads and a little silver amulet. The amulet was a strip of silver that had been rolled up, then probably worn around someone's neck on a chain or cord as a "good luck charm."

The silver was so old and fragile that the experts took two or three years to decide how to treat the silver so they could unroll the amulet without destroying it. When the amulet was finally unrolled, it proved to be a strip of silver about seven inches long and an inch wide, and engraved on the silver in very tiny letters they found the priestly blessing from Numbers 6:24-26:

"The Lord bless you and keep you;
The Lord make his face to shine upon you, and be gracious to you;
The Lord lift up his countenance upon you, and give you peace."

This amulet is now the oldest fragment of Scripture that has ever been discovered. Prior to its discovery, the Dead Sea Scrolls were our oldest biblical manuscripts (and some of them go back to 150-200 B.C.), but the silver amulet is 400 to 500 years older than the Scrolls. The amulet is a priceless discovery — so significant that the amulet and the ivory pomegranate from Solomon's Temple are the only two artifacts displayed in a large, newly-opened room in the Israel Museum in Jerusalem.

Chapter Four

The Life of Christ

Bill Humble:

It's been 2,000 years since Jesus lived and died here in the Bible land. That is a long time and many changes have taken place. Cities where Jesus lived and preached are now buried under the debris of the ages.

One of the values of archaeology is to locate these sites, excavate them, and allow us to stand again where Jesus once stood.

Let's begin with His birth. We know He was born in Bethlehem. But where in Bethlehem? Justin Martyr in the second century wrote about the cave where Jesus was born, a cave that once served as the stable under an inn.

Queen Helena came here in the fourth century and she ordered a church built over the cave. The cave is still here, and archaeologists have found part of the mosaic floor of that original church.

These mosaics are 1,600 years old, and they show us something of the beauty of that first great church built on this site.

After Helena's church was destroyed, the emperor Justinian built a new church on the same site in 533, and this is the Church of the Nativity that still stands today — one of the oldest churches in the Christian world.

The low entrance was built after the crusades to keep looters from driving their carts into the church.

It's a beautiful old church, with gold chandeliers and a Greek Orthodox altar. Ostrich eggs hang over the altar.

Elias Subeh:

This tradition goes back to the fourth century. They say the ostrich watches for her egg to be hatched, looking straight to the egg, so the Lord is watching us, what we are giving to the church. So that's why the Eastern Church keeps the ostrich egg right in front of the main altar.

Bill Humble:

The cave that Justin Martyr wrote about is under the church, and the traditional place of Jesus' birth is now marked by a silver star.

Elias Subeh:

When we talk about an inn like a Hilton or Sheraton or Holiday Inn, in that time if they wanted to build a deluxe hotel, they must have a cave underneath where they could keep the animals. So that's how it happened that the King of kings was born in stable among the animals when He could have been born in a royal palace.

Bill Humble:

Jesus grew up in Nazareth, but when He began His public ministry, He went to Capernaum and the area around the Sea of Galilee.

Archaeologists have done a lot of work at Capernaum, and a century ago they began uncovering a beautiful synagogue made of white limestone. The native stone around Capernaum is black basalt, and that's what the people used to build their houses. So the limestone for the synagogue had to be brought from somewhere else, and it stood in sharp contrast with the black houses around it.

The synagogue is 70 feet long, and it is decorated with beautiful columns. The seating was on stone benches around the walls. This decoration, carved in stone, may be a picture of the ark of the covenant as some artist envisioned it. Scholars think that this synagogue was built in the third or fourth century, so it was not there in Jesus' day.

However, archaeologists have recently found the foundations of an earlier synagogue that stood on the same site. Notice the black stone. This was probably the foundation of the synagogue where Jesus taught so often.

A hundred yards east of the synagogue, archaeologists have recently been at work, using American college students, and they have uncovered many more buildings for first-century Capernaum.

John Wilson and Vassilios Tzaferis describe their work:

John Wilson:

What, in your estimate, is the greatest value of what we have done here on this site?

Vassilios Tzaferis:

On this site, though we didn't discover a magnificent synagogue and churches, we discovered the houses, the streets and public buildings that were here in Jesus' time during the Roman period.

Bill Humble:

These excavations have shown that Capernaum was a larger and more important city than scholars had realized. And they have shown that there was a strong Roman presence here, as evidenced by the discovery of a large Roman bath only a few yards from the Sea of Galilee.

The most exciting discovery in these excavations was gold — the largest hoard of ancient gold coins ever found in Israel.

John Wilson:

It's hard to tell you what kind of excitement develops on a site like this when gold is discovered — 282 gold dinars, lots of gold, twenty-two carats, pure gold. I hate to keep saying archaeology is not hunting for treasure. People say, "Did you find anything?" We found the history of an ancient people and that's what we were looking for. But once in a while it's fun to find a treasure, too, and that's what we did here.

Bill Humble:

Chorazin was about two miles north of Capernaum up in the Galilean hills, and its synagogue was made out of the native black stone — not limestone like Capernaum. Chorazin is one of the cities Jesus condemned for its unbelief.

Here is an interesting find from the synagogue at Chorazin — Moses' seat. When Jesus talked about the scribes sitting on Moses' seat, it was not a figurative expression. Each synagogue had a seat where the scribes sat and taught the Law.

Many buildings are now being uncovered at Chorazin, and they are all made of the same black stone.

Archaeology has often been of value in locating sites connected with the life of Jesus. As early as the third century, Christians believed that one of Jesus' miracles, sending the evil spirits into the herd of swine, happened here at Kursi on the northeast shore of the Sea of Galilee. And in the fifth or sixth century a great church was built here. But that church was buried and forgotten until 1970, when it was discovered by accident. They were building a new road through here and uncovered the ruins of that church.

Vassilios Tzaferis excavated the church, and he tells us about it.

Vassilios Tzaferis:

Only after three months excavation a unique discovery was found — an enormous Christian basilica from the fifth or sixth century A.D., set up in the middle of a large monastery. Now the topography of the place and the site make it the site of the swine miracle, and there is no doubt about it. Archaeology does not prove that the miracle took place, but it says that Christians from the fifth century saw in that place the place of the miracle.

Bill Humble:

There are large sections of the mosaic floor of the church that are still intact. The mosaics have a geometric design with the flowers and birds of the region.

Up on the hillside above the church, there is an ancient tower built over a large boulder 22 feet high. The early Christians believed this was the exact spot where the miracle took place.

Beth Shan was one of the 10 Greek cities called "the Decapolis," and we learn in Mark 7 that Jesus once left Galilee and traveled in Decapolis — perhaps around Beth Shan, since it was the only one of the 10 cities on the west bank of the Jordan River.

Beth Shan was a great Canaanite city in Old Testament times and was located up on the tell. When Saul and Jonathan were killed, their bodies were hung on the city wall here. But in Jesus' day the Roman city of Beth Shan lay at the base of the tell, and this city is now being excavated for the first time.

The archaeologists are finding many impressive buildings from Jesus' day. They have found a Roman street lined with columns on both sides. This capital shows the magnificence of that city. They are finding well-preserved mosaics in many of the buildings.

Beth Shan. Tell of ancient city in the distance.

Across the ruins of the city, we see a Roman theater that was built around 200 A.D. that seated 5,000 people. The theater was excavated 50 years ago and is the best-preserved theater anywhere in the Bible land.

Elias Subeh:
This is the only theater in the Holy Land that was used for execution. That's where they used to bring Christians and throw them to the lions here.

Bill Humble:
There was a strong Roman army presence in the area of Beth Shan. They are now uncovering a large Roman bath with the typical caldarium or hot room. The little columns made of brick supported a floor, and hot air was forced up around these columns into the bath.

The Roman Sixth Legion had a camp just south of Beth Shan, and 10 years ago a bronze bust of the Emperor Hadrian was found in this camp. Hadrian was the emperor who destroyed Jerusalem the second time in 132 A.D. and provoked the Bar Kochba rebellion. This is one of the most beautiful busts of an emperor ever found. Notice the breastplate with its mythological battle.

As Jesus went through Decapolis and Galilee, He walked on Roman roads that were marked with Roman mileposts.

Joseph Shulam:
During the Roman period the Romans put milestones on all major highways that they built. And here a few have survived from the Roman period. This one is still legible. It has Caesarea mentioned

here on the top and Jerusalem below it and other ancient cities of the Near East.

Bill Humble:

As Jesus and His disciples traveled over the land, they would have passed many milestones like these — each one a reminder of the Roman control of their land.

One time, as they were traveling through Samaria, they came to the valley between Ebal and Gerezim and stopped at Jacob's well.

This is Jacob's well. This well was here in the days of Jesus, perhaps in the days of Jacob 1,500 years earlier. One time Jesus and His disciples left Jerusalem, came through Samaria, arrived here at noon. Jesus sat down at this well and the disciples went into town to find something to eat. The Samaritan woman came. Jesus asked her for drink, and she was surprised that He, a Jew, would even speak to her. Then Jesus told her that He would give her living water, and she said, "Sir, you have nothing to draw with, and the well is deep" — and it still is. And it was here that Jesus said to the woman, "God is spirit, and they that worship him must worship in spirit and in truth."

At the end of His three-year ministry, Jesus came to Jerusalem for the last time and was crucified — somewhere outside the walls of old Jerusalem. We know from historians like Josephus that the Romans crucified thousands of people. But no archaeological evidence of crucifixion had ever been found until Vassilios Tzaferis made a grim discovery.

Vassilios Tzaferis:

It happened in Jerusalem after the Six Days War when we started excavating around Jerusalem and I excavated a lot of tombs. So in one of them I found a Jewish tomb with many ossuaries of the first century A.D. — exactly the time of Christ. And in one ossuary were found the bones of a Jew who was named Yehohanan [John], and both his ankles were pierced by an iron nail of 15 centimeters long. And after examination of the bones, it was found this poor person was crucified, and for the first time we have a real archaeological evidence showing how people were crucified. But from the time of Jesus, we had no archaeological evidence, and it came just in time.

Bill Humble:

What about the new tomb of Joseph of Arimathea where Jesus was buried? Have archaeologists found it?

The Church of the Holy Sepulchre probably stands on the site of that tomb. What we can know, for sure, is that the Emperor Constantine built a great church on this site in the fourth century, and there are remains of that basilica in the present Crusader church. Inside the church there is an outcropping of rock that might be Golgotha, the place of execution.

But when Constantine built his church in the fourth century, the tomb of Jesus was already gone. The Emperor Hadrian had destroyed it in 132 A.D. and had built a pagan temple on the site.

So even if the Holy Sepulchre does not mark the place where Jesus was buried, it bears no resemblance to His tomb. And with six rival churches fighting over who will control the site, a Catholic archaeologist has written, "The empty who come to be filled will leave desolate."

Dark and gloomy, the church is probably an authentic site that is covered over with 1,500 years of

Christian devotion and superstition. And it does little to bring the Bible to life.

Garden tomb in Jerusalem.

Many visitors to Jerusalem find the Garden Tomb far more impressive than the Church of the Holy Sepulchre. It's an ancient tomb, just north of the Damascus Gate, and when we see this tomb, still set in a garden, the gospel story of resurrection comes alive.

William White explains:

William White:

We do not claim that this is the tomb where the Lord Jesus was buried, but as a visual aid to the Easter story I believe it is a meaningful place. We at the Garden Tomb are reticent about being too dogmatic because some people tend to overemphasize the problems of discovering New Testament sites in Jerusalem. For us the person must always be more important than the place, because the Savior is more important than the site.

Bill Humble:

The gospel of John says that Jesus' tomb was in a garden, and the Garden Tomb shows us what an ancient tomb set in a garden was like. They have found an ancient winepress at the Garden Tomb, and this shows that there was a garden, or a vineyard, near the tomb.

It is an authentic ancient tomb cut into the solid rock, a Jewish tomb that goes back to the time of the first century. And notice the stone trough along in front of the tomb where a large circular stone would be rolled back and forth to seal this tomb. The large stone here at the Garden Tomb is gone.

But just west of old walled Jerusalem there is another ancient tomb. It has four large rooms underground and was probably built by Herod the Great for his family. And here, the large rolling stone is still in place.

When we see the size and weight of this stone, the New Testament story comes alive and we can feel the concern of the women: "Who can roll the stone away?"

The Garden Tomb takes us back to the New Testament and to the women who came to the tomb and found it empty. It gives us a picture of what the tomb of Jesus was like, and it renews our faith in a living Jesus.

And let's remember that archaeology has identified

many authentic sites connected with the life of Jesus, and this makes His life and ministry real to us.

But let's remember that the ultimate truths of Christianity are beyond the reach of archaeology. There's no way that archaeology could ever prove that He was God or that He was raised from the dead.

Even if the real tomb of Jesus could be found, just like it was the day he laid there, it would be empty. Archaeology could never explain what happened to His body. Only faith can say He is risen. The discoveries of archaeology are of great value, but our faith lies beyond archaeology.

Scriptures for Study

Luke 2:1-21; Matthew 1:18-2:12. Birth of Jesus.

Luke 4:31-39; Matthew 4:12-25. Ministry at Capernaum.

Luke 7:1-10. A healing at Capernaum with a reference to the synagogue.

John 4:1-42. Samaritan woman at Jacob's Well.

John 19:38-42; Matthew 27:57-66. Jesus' tomb.

Notes from Archaeology

The Church at Kursi

The church at Kursi is a good example of how important archaeological discoveries are often made by accident. Kursi is located on the northeast shore of the Sea of Galilee, opposite Capernaum, which is on the northwest shore. In 1970 the Israelis were building a new road through the Golan Heights, and as a bulldozer worked near the shore of the Sea of Galilee, it began to turn up many pieces of Byzantine pottery and then the ruins of an ancient building.

Israeli law requires that when this happens on a construction project, work must be halted until the Department of Antiquities can examine the site.

Archaeologist Vassilios Tzaferis was called to the Kursi site, and after three months of excavation, he determined that the ruins were a large Byzantine church. Work continued at the site for five seasons (1970-1973 and 1980) and uncovered the well-preserved ruins of a large monastery with a church inside the monastery.

The church marked the site where early Christians believed to have taken place Jesus' miracle of sending the Gardarene demoniac into the herd of swine. This miracle is recorded in all three Synoptic Gospels (Matthew 8:28-34; Mark 5:1-20; and Luke 8:26-39). According to these accounts the demon-possessed man wandered naked among the tombs and had such strength that he broke the chains of those who attempted to capture him. When Jesus commanded the demons to leave the man, they begged to enter a herd of swine, whereupon the 2,000 swine rushed down a steep bank and were drowned in the sea.

As early as the third century, the early Christian fathers identified Kursi as the place where this *remarkable* miracle had taken place. Then, in the fifth or sixth century, the monastery and church were built on the site. The Persian invasion of the Bible land in 614 A.D. and the Muslim conquest a few years later ended Christian pilgrimages to Kursi. The church was destroyed by a disastrous earthquake in 747 A.D., and over the centuries the ruins were covered with sand and dirt. The site was forgotten until the Israeli bulldozer began turning up pottery in 1970.

Tzaferis found that the architecture of the church was typical of a Byzantine basilica from the sixth century. It had a central nave with columns on either side to separate the nave from the aisles. At the end of the nave there was a semicircular apse. Rooms on either side of the nave were used for various purposes. One had an olive-press, which shows that the production of olive oil provided income for the monastic community. Archaeologist Tzaferis also found a burial crypt and a baptistry. Originally, the church's whole floor was covered with tile mosaics. Set in a geometric pattern, the mosaics pictured the flowers and birds of the region. However, after the Muslims conquered the Bible land, they destroyed many of the mosaics because the Koran forbade art that pictured humans or animals. But about 60 percent of the mosaics are still intact and are a beautiful example of this Byzantine art form.

The Kursi church lies at the foot of a steep hill. Halfway up the hill Tzaferis found the ruins of an ancient tower with walls 3 feet thick. When the tower was excavated in 1980, it was found that the lower part enclosed a huge boulder 22 feet high, which was the exact spot where early Christians believed the swine miracle was performed. The upper part of the tower had a small chapel with a colorful mosaic floor.

There is no way that archaeology could ever prove that the swine miracle took place. But as Tzaferis has emphasized, the excavations at Kursi do prove that the early Christians believed this steep hillside, overlooking the Sea of Galilee, was where it happened.

The Crucifixion of John

Ancient historians record the agonizing death of thousands of people on crosses, but no archaeological evidence of crucifixion had ever been found — until 1968.

Crucifixion was first practiced in the East among the Assyrians and Persians long before the days of the Roman Empire. The Jews knew about crucifixion and found it loathsome. According to Deuteronomy 21:22,23, if a man was to be put to death and was hanged on a tree, the body had to be removed and buried the same day: "For a hanged man is accursed by God; you shall not defile your land which the Lord your God gives you for an inheritance." But when the Jews fell under the control of the Hellenistic Ptolemy and Seleucid rulers (after Alexander the Great's death in 323 B.C.), crucifixion was often used as a mode of execution, and sometimes even by their own Maccabean kings.

Near the end of the first century B.C., the Romans adopted crucifixion as a punishment for slaves. At first it was used for punishment, not execution, so the slave would be scourged and tied, not nailed, to a cross and left to hang in agony for many hours. Later the Romans began using the cross as a method of executing slaves, rebels and foreign captives. Sometimes there were mass crucifixions. After the Romans crushed Spartacus' revolt in 71 B.C., they crucified 6,000 rebels. When Titus had Jerusalem under siege in 70 A.D., the Roman army crucified hundreds of Jews a day; this went on for several months.

But no tangible archaeological evidence of a single crucifixion had ever been found — until 1968, when Vassilios Tzaferis made a grim discovery on Mount Scopus near Jerusalem. The Six Days War in 1967 opened many areas for excavation, and Tzaferis was excavating a number of Jewish tombs from the first century. One of the tombs contained eight ossuaries filled with bones. An ossuary is a "bone box," usually about two feet long and made of limestone or marble, which was used in a distinctive Jewish burial custom. After a body had been in a tomb long enough for the flesh to decay and disappear, the bones would be collected and given a permanent burial in the same tomb in an ossuary. This allowed the tomb to be used generation after generation. The custom of secondary burial began during the time of Herod the Great and continued for about 200 years.

One of the ossuaries Tzaferis found in the tomb on Mount Scopus contained the bones of a Jewish man about 25 years old, who died during the first century A.D. The man's name, engraved on the ossuary, was Jehohanan (John). He must have belonged to a fairly prominent Jewish family, for another ossuary had the inscription, "Simon, builder of the Temple" — evidently a member of the family who had worked in Herod the Great's rebuilding of the temple. When the bones of Jehohanan were examined, it was found that a seven-inch-long iron nail had been driven through his two ankle bones. Jehohanan had died on a cross!

Earlier medical studies of crucifixion had shown that when a victim was crucified, breathing soon became very difficult. The victim would try to support his body by pushing up on his nail-pierced feet, would gasp for air, and then die of suffocation within two or three hours. The Roman executioners learned that they could prolong the agony by nailing a little seat called a *sedile* on the front of the cross. The *sedile* was pointed to intensify the pain, but with this body support, the victim sometimes lingered for two or three days. The little seat may explain a common Roman phrase, "to sit on a cross."

According to Tzaferis, when experts examined Jehohanan's bones, they concluded that he had been crucified on a cross with a *sedile.* But because of the way the single nail had penetrated both ankle bones, they also concluded that Jehohanan had been crucified in a twisted contorted position. If his arms were nailed to the cross, then his legs were twisted around at a 90-degree angle and held together as a single nail was driven through both ankles into the cross. Twisted in agony, John hung on his cross until death came; this may have been within a few years of the time when Jesus died on his cross.

The ankle bones of John, still pierced with the seven-inch nail, are a grim picture of what Jesus suffered on Golgotha, and they are the only tangible archaeological evidence of crucifixion that has ever been discovered.

(This information about crucifixion is from the author's interview of Vassilios Tzaferis and from Tzaferis' article, "Crucifixion — The Archaeological Evidence," in *Biblical Archaeology Review,* Jan./Feb. 1985.)

CHAPTER FIVE

The Jerusalem Jesus Knew

Bill Humble:

Jerusalem has been the focal point of Bible history from the time of David and Solomon, about a thousand years before Christ down to the death of Jesus and the establishment of His church. The temple of Solomon once stood on Mount Moriah where the Dome of the Rock stands today, and the cross of Jesus once stood somewhere just outside the wall of the city. Jerusalem has been attacked and besieged many, many times, destroyed again and again, and for this reason there have been many archaeological discoveries that help us understand the history of Jerusalem and its relation to the Bible.

We want to spend most of our time in first-century Jerusalem where Jesus walked. But let's begin 4,000 years ago in the days of Abraham and Sarah.

When Abraham met Melchizedek, king of Salem or Jerusalem, the city was very small, and it was located on the hill Ophel, south of the present walled city.

The area is now called "the city of David," and excavations by Kathleen Kenyon have shown that this early city that David captured lay entirely outside the present south wall.

After David captured Jerusalem, he bought a threshing floor on Mount Moriah to the north, and there Solomon built the temple — where the Dome of the Rock now stands.

Under the kings of Judah, Jerusalem grew to the west, then was destroyed by Nebuchadnezzar in 587 B.C., and then rebuilt after the return from Babylonian exile.

What did Jerusalem look like in Jesus' day 2,000 years ago? Think how the Bible would spring to life if we could walk through the Jerusalem that Jesus knew. Thankfully, we can. Archaeologists and historians have built a scale model of first-century Jerusalem, 1/50 the real size. This shows us the Jerusalem that Herod built, the Jerusalem that Jesus knew, the Jerusalem destroyed by the Roman army in 70 A.D.

Jerusalem was located on the crest of the Judean hills 2,500 feet above sea level. Herod the Great had done vast building work all over the city, but the temple on Mount Moriah was its glory.

On the opposite side of the city, to the west, Herod had built a magnificent palace. It had two main buildings, and each one had banquet halls and bedrooms for hundreds of guests. There was a large courtyard between the two buildings with groves of trees, fountains and bronze sculptures pouring water into the fountains.

The palace was protected by walls and towers on every side, including the east side where it faced the city. At the north end of the palace, there were three great towers to guard the palace and the city.

The largest was the Tower of Phasael named for Herod's brother. It was 148 feet tall. The bottom part of the tower was solid stone work, and this is still standing today. The top part was a small palace — an ancient penthouse.

The second tower was named Hippicus for a friend of Herod. It also had rooms on the top and was 132 feet tall.

The third tower, 75 feet tall, was named for Herod's wife, Mariamne. Herod loved her madly, but when she was accused of unfaithfulness, he had her put to death, then almost went mad because of what he had done. The rooms in this tower were more luxurious than the other two, as befitted a Queen.

There was an army barracks between the three towers and the palace. When the Romans destroyed Jerusalem, some of the heaviest fighting was around the three towers. Herod was right in thinking that an attack on Jerusalem would probably come from the north.

Just east of the palace was a large open area surrounded by shops and colonnades, called the Upper Market. The area around the market was the Upper City. This is the part of Jerusalem where the homes of the wealthy were located. A deep valley separated the Upper City from the temple mount.

The largest palace in the Upper City belonged to the Maccabees, the Jewish royal family who ruled the Jews for a hundred years before the Romans took over. This palace had two towers and a courtyard along with living quarters and baths.

The Upper City also had a theater that Herod had built — another evidence of his love for the culture of Greece and Rome.

When Herod began making plans to rebuild the temple, he found that Mount Moriah was not big enough for the temple he wanted to build. So Herod built an enormous retaining wall around the temple mount and filled it in with rocks and earth, so this platform became the site for his temple.

At the southeast corner, the great retaining wall was 211 feet high and came to be called "the pinnacle of the temple." One of Jesus' temptations — "Cast yourself down" — may have taken place here.

At the south wall, there was a great flight of steps leading up to the wall with its two gates, the Huldah Gates. The tomb of the prophetess Huldah was in front of the steps. From these gates there were stairs, through large tunnels, going up to the temple.

On the west side the Tyropoeon Valley (also called the Cheesemaker's Valley) separated the temple mount from the Upper City. There was a bridge across this valley from the Upper City to the temple.

And at the southwest corner of the temple mount, a wide stairway went down from the temple to a street in the valley below.

The summit of Mount Moriah was a large open court, called the "Court of the Gentiles," 1,300 feet long and 700 feet wide. It had colonnaded porticos on all four sides.

The Royal Portico, on the south, was twice as large as the others. As we look through its columns, we can visualize the stalls with sacrificial animals for sale, the money-changers, and the rabbis teaching their students.

Solomon's portico, where Jesus often met with His disciples, was on the east.

There was a large wall, called the balastrade, that separated the temple proper from the Court of the Gentiles. The balastrade had 13 gates, and each one had a sign warning Gentiles that they could not go into the temple on pain of death. And archaeologists have actually found one of those warning signs.

The first court of the temple was the "Court of the Women," and as the name suggests, Jewish women were allowed into this court. One corner of this court was set aside for people making Nazarite vows, another for the purification of lepers.

The Nicanor Gate led from the Court of the Women to the Court of the Israelites, where Jewish men could go. This beautiful gate was made of copper. It was approached by 15 curved steps, where the Levites sang and played.

The temple itself was as tall as a 15-story building. It was made out of three kinds of marble. The two columns on the front, patterned after Solomon's temple, were reddish marble. The sides of the temple were of white marble, the foundation, blue. The huge door was 65 feet high.

It was decorated with gold around the top. According to Josephus, the temple looked like a snowy-white mountain glittering in the sunshine.

Herod built a large fortress at the northwest corner of the temple mountain and named it Antonio in honor of Mark Antony. From the towers at Herod's palace, we can see the fortress in the distance.

The fortress had towers over 100 feet tall at the four corners, with large gates on the east and west, and another gate going into the Court of the Gentiles.

Inside the fortress there were two large courtyards paved with stones, with cloisters and barracks surrounding the courtyards.

When a mob tried to kill Paul in Acts 21, he was rescued by soldiers and taken into this fortress. And Jesus may have been condemned to death here.

The Pool of Bethesda was just north of the fortress, with the sheep market near the pool.

Just south of the temple mount, Herod had built a Roman-style hippodrome, or stadium. It was used for chariot races in spite of the Jews' hostility to such a sport. The floor of the stadium had a wall and turning posts, and the chariots raced around these. Seating was about like a modern football stadium.

Just below the hippodrome there was a row of palaces along the city wall. And below the palaces, the Synagogue of the Freedmen where Stephen preached and became the first Christian martyr.

The Pool of Siloam was near the synagogue. This is where the Hezekiah tunnel brought water from the Gihon Spring into the city, and it is where Jesus healed the blind man in John 9. Above the pool, the lower city is where many of the poor lived.

Golgotha, the place of execution, was outside the city on the west, not far from Herod's three towers. If Pilate condemned Jesus to death in the fortress Antonio (as many believe), it was only a few hundred yards, straight west, to the rocky hill where He died.

The Jerusalem that Jesus knew came to an end in 70 A.D., destroyed and burned by the Roman army under Titus. But even so, archaeology has identified many sites from Jesus' day.

The Romans destroyed the temple completely, but not the large retaining wall around the temple mountain. The Western Wall is still standing and the massive Herodian stones are still in place. This is the Jews' holiest shrine and they come here for prayer. The young orthodox come, and the old. Soldiers pray at the wall.

On special days like Pentecost and Jerusalem Day, thousands come to the wall for their morning prayers, wearing prayer shawls and phylactories. They come before dawn, and the prayers go on for many hours.

Judge Steven Adler, who sits on the National Labor Court of Israel, tells us what the wall means to him:

Steven Adler:

I think for me that archaeology and the different things that are found in the archaeological digs are important because they show me in a physical way, an actual way, the things that existed in the time of the Bible. It's mentioned that people would come up to Jerusalem from all over the country to pray at the temple wall, and today this happens, too. People from all over Jerusalem and even all over Israel come to the Western Wall and pray at the Western Wall, and this makes the Bible real, makes it alive, and this is what is so exciting about Jerusalem and the archaeology here.

Bill Humble:

Jewish women have their own section of the wall, and they're not allowed at the men's section.

Judge Adler tells us about the phylactories and about a discovery at Masada.

Steven Adler:

The Jew prays three times a day. When he prays in the morning, he wears these phylactories, one on the arm and one on the head. The one on the arm is pointed at the heart, from the Bible injunction to keep God all the time in your heart, and the one on the head is right between the eyes because of the injunction to keep God in your mind all the time. And they are put on with straps on the arm. If you go to the Museum in Jerusalem, you'll see that at Masada they found phylactories which are the same type and have the same biblical script and inside the little boxes, the script, "Hear, O Israel, the Lord our God is one," and these were found inside the boxes at Masada.

Bill Humble:

At the south end of the Western Wall, in Jesus' day, there was a wide stairway that led down into the valley. And archaeologists have found the place where that stairway was anchored to the ancient wall. And these are the foundations where the stairway came down to the valley. Remains of the ancient Herodian street through the valley can still be seen.

The south wall in Jesus' day had a broad flight of steps leading up to the Huldah gates. This wall has been excavated by Benjamin Mazar over the last 10 years. Notice the beautiful condition of these stones. The margin around each stone is hardly worn. The reason is that these stones had been buried ever since the year 70 A.D.

Look at the size of this enormous stone — 6 feet high and 27 feet long. It weighs over 200 tons, and there are other Herodian stones in the wall that are twice this size.

Today we can walk down the broad steps at the south wall. Some of these are the original steps. Jesus might have walked into the temple on these very steps.

The southwest corner of the temple mount was called "the place of trumpeting" in Jesus' day. We know from Josephus that a priest stood here and sounded a trumpet across the upper city to announce the beginning of Sabbath.

Archaeologists recently dug up a stone three feet wide here. It has an inscription, and it reads, "Place of Trumpeting." When the temple was destroyed in 70 A.D., this stone fell from the corner high above and was buried here ever since.

The Phasael Tower stood at the north end of Herod the Great's palace. The base of that tower, 30 feet high, is still standing in the Citadel.

The Pool of Siloam provided a water supply for Herodian Jerusalem. And today we can still wade through Hezekiah's tunnel, and we come out of the tunnel at the Pool of Siloam.

This beautiful view of Jerusalem is from Mount Scopus, and, according to Josephus, Vespasian planned his siege of the city from here on Mount Scopus. The siege finally came to an end with the city destroyed under Titus in August of 70 A.D.

Archaeologists have recently found a house destroyed at that time, and this is the first archaeological evidence of Jerusalem's fall. The house belonged to an important priestly family named Kathros.

The archaeologists found vivid evidence of the destruction — broken pottery and furniture and the charred beams that fell from the ceiling. They even found the skeleton of a young woman who was killed by the Romans on that awful day.

The wealthy families lived in the upper city around the Maccabean palace in Jesus' day. Archaeologists working in this area have recently found a large Herodian villa destroyed in 70 A.D. This villa is so large and luxurious that the archaeologists think it might have been the home of Ananias, the high priest at the time Jerusalem was destroyed. The villa was opened to the public as a museum in 1989.

The basement area of the villa is well-preserved with a water system, ritual baths, and several floors that are decorated with mosaics. The villa had beautiful plastered walls. One of the walls was decorated to look like Herodian stones with the margin cut around each stone. First-century furniture was found, including this pedestal table and this glass bowl.

A long wooden beam had fallen across a mosaic floor and burned, and archaeologists left the charred wood and ashes in place — grim evidence of the terrible destruction that came to Jerusalem in August of 70 A.D.

Thanks to the many discoveries of archaeology, the Jerusalem of today melts into the Jerusalem of the past — where Abraham met Melchizedek, where Solomon built God's temple, and where Jesus preached and died. Thanks to archaeology there is no spot on earth where the Bible is more real than in Jerusalem.

Scriptures for Study

2 Samuel 5:1-12. David captures Jerusalem.

John 2:13-25. Jesus cleanses the temple.

Matthew 23:37-39. Lament over Jerusalem.

Luke 19:28-47; John 12:12-19. Jesus' triumphal entry into Jerusalem.

Matthew 26:47–27:66; John 18-19. Jesus' arrest, trials and crucifixion.

Acts 21:17-40. Paul assaulted in temple.

Notes from Archaeology

The Model City

The Model City, showing Jerusalem as it was in 66 A.D. shortly before its destruction by the Roman army, is located on the grounds of the Holyland Hotel in southwest Jerusalem. The late Professor Avi-Yonah of Hebrew University in Jerusalem compiled the historical and archaeological data that was used for building the model city. The materials used were, as far as possible, the same materials that would have been used in the first century: limestone, marble, wood, iron, copper, etc. Whenever archaeologists discover new information about ancient Jerusalem, the Model City is changed to conform to the new insights.

When people see pictures of the Model City, they usually ask, "How big is the model? And how accurate is it?" The model is on a scale of one to 50, so the city is about one-third as long as a football field. The tallest buildings in ancient Jerusalem were the temple and the towers at Herod's palace, and since these were about 150 feet high, they are 3 feet high in the model. The city wall is about 18 inches high. If there were "model people" walking around the city, they would be about an inch-and-a-half high.

Antonio Fortress in the Model City. Holyland Hotel in Jerusalem.

How accurate is the Model City? As accurate as current archaeological and historical information allow. Scholars used every possible source of information in planning the model: the Talmud, Mishna, Josephus, the New Testament and data provided by archaeology. However, detailed information about ancient buildings — where they were and what they looked like — is often not available. For example, Josephus informs us that Herod the Great built an amphitheater or hippodrome for chariot races south of the temple mountain. But no archaeological trace of this hippodrome has ever been found. So, relying on information about what ancient hippodromes looked like, the model city has a hippodrome south of the temple, but this in only a guess as to what Herod's structure was like.

However, remains of many ancient structures still survive, such as Herod's great retaining wall around the temple mountain; and whenever this is true, there is little doubt about the accuracy of the Model City.

Excavations Around the Wall

The ancient writers often speak of the beauty and magnificence of the Jerusalem that Herod the Great had built. The Roman scholar Pliny says that Jerusalem was "by far the most renowned city of the Orient." The Talmud tells us that "whoever has not seen Jerusalem in its splendor has never seen a lovely city." And Josephus says that the royal portico on the temple mount was "more worthy of description than any other structure under the sun."

The crowning glory of Herodian Jerusalem was the temple on Mount Moriah and the great retaining wall around the temple mount. As Herod planned the rebuilding of the Second Temple, he realized that Mount Moriah was not large enough to accommodate his grandiose plans. So he built an enormous retaining wall around the temple mount, 200 feet high at the southeast corner, and filled it in with rocks and dirt up to the level of the mountaintop. This became the platform for the temple and the columned porticos that surrounded it on every side.

When Jerusalem fell to the Romans in 70 A.D., the temple was totally destroyed, but not the great wall around Mount Moriah. Large sections of this wall are still intact. Today, the Dome of the Rock stands on the summit of the temple mount where the temple stood in Jesus' day. The Dome is Muslim, the oldest Muslim shrine on earth. The Muslim armies conquered Jerusalem in 638 A.D., and the Dome of the Rock was begun about a half-century later — then the El Aksa Mosque. The Dome is such a holy site of Muslims (only Mecca and Medina are holier) that no archaeological work has ever been allowed on the temple mount.

Nor were excavations allowed at the retaining wall around the temple mount prior to 1967. The old city of Jerusalem is located in the West Bank, and the West Bank was part of Jordan from the United Nations' establishment of Israel in 1948 until 1967. Then the Jews' total victory over their Arab neighbors in the Six Days War brought the entire West Bank under Israeli control. This opened the door for Israeli archaeologists to begin work in old Jerusalem (except on the temple mount, which they dare not touch). So, in 1968, Benjamin Mazar began a decade of excavation at the south wall of the temple mount.

The principal entrance to the temple in Jesus' day was at the south wall. There was a large plaza below the wall where throngs of worshipers gathered for such festivals as Passover, Pentecost and Tabernacles. A magnificent flight of steps 200 feet wide led from the plaza to two sets of gates (called the Huldah

Gates in the Mishnah). After entering these gates, worshipers climbed flights of steps, through large tunnels, up to the summit of Mount Moriah where the temple stood. Over the centuries many feet of earth and debris had accumulated along the wall, and when Mazar removed this debris, he found the Huldah Gates and the steps leading up to the wall. Since the lower courses of Herodian stones in the wall had been buried for many centuries, the margin cut around each stone was well-preserved. These stones give us a picture of what the entire wall, nearly 200 feet high, looked like in Jesus' day. Mazar uncovered stones of enormous size, one 27 feet long that weighed at least 200 tons.

Thousands of Jews gather at the Western Wall on Pentecost morning.

Mazar found a stone at the southwest corner of the temple mount with an inscription reading, "The place of trumpeting." This stone had marked the place, high above the temple mountain, where a priest stood every Sabbath and sounded a trumpet across the Upper City to announce the beginning of the Sabbath. It fell when the Romans destroyed the temple and had been buried ever since.

Nearly 300 feet south of the Huldah Gates, Mazar found the ruins of a large Herodian building. But what was even more important, the archaeologists found that the Herodian building had been built atop the ruins of a large building from the seventh or eighth centuries B.C. They believe this was the structure called "Beth Millo" in 2 Kings 12:22, where King Josiah was murdered. The Beth Millo was destroyed when Nebuchadnezzar took Jerusalem in 587 B.C.

The Western Wall of the temple mountain (often called the "Wailing Wall" by non-Jews) has been the Jews' holiest shrine for many centuries. They were denied access to the Western Wall when old Jerusalem was in Jordan (1948-1967), but since the Six Days War they have come to the Western Wall for prayers, just as the people of Israel did in Old Testament days. There have been recent excavations in the Rabbinic Tunnel to try to determine how far the Western Wall extends to the north. They have found a Herodian stone weighing an estimated 415 tons in this tunnel. It is hard to visualize ancient stone masons with crude tools cutting stones of such enormous size, and then moving them from the quarry a half-mile away to the spot where they would be placed in Herod's wall. But somehow they did it.

What has been the value of these excavations around the temple mount? Benjamin Mazar has written, "During the entire Herodian period the area around the Temple Mount was the center of public life in Jerusalem and a focal point for the masses of Jerusalemites and pilgrims who came to offer their sacrifices at the Holy Temple." And he adds that the magnificence of the temple mount, as revealed in his excavations, "fully supports the splendor described in the ancient literary sources." No wonder Jesus' disciples found it almost unbelievable when He foretold that not one stone would be left standing on another.

Warning Stone Inscription

The balastrade was a large wall that enclosed the temple and separated it from the large court of the Gentiles around it. The balastrade had 13 gates where Jews went into the temple, and at each gate there was a stone that forbade Gentiles to enter the temple.

In 1871 a French archaeologist, Charles Clermont-Ganneau, discovered one of the warning stones from the balastrade. The inscription is in Greek and says, "Let no one of the Gentiles enter inside the barrier around the sanctuary and the porch, and if he transgresses, he shall himself bear the blame for his ensuing death." It was a capital offense for a Gentile to go into the temple. The warning stone is now on display in the Istanbul Museum.

Archaeologists found another of the warning stones, this one fragmentary, in excavations near St. Stephen's Gate in Jerusalem in 1935.

These warning stones help us understand the gravity of the accusations against Paul: "Men of Israel, help! This is the man . . . who brought Greeks into the temple, and he has defiled this holy place" (Acts 21:28). The aroused mob would have killed

Paul on the spot had not the Roman troops rescued him and escorted him out of the Court of the Gentiles into the Fortress Antonio.

Clermont-Ganneau, who found the first warning stone, is also credited with securing the famous Moabite Stone for the Louvre in Paris in 1870. The Moabite Stone goes back to about 840-820 B.C. and has a lengthy inscription in which King Mesha of Moab describes how he paid tribute to Israel, and then, with the help of his god Chemosh, revolted against King Ahab and Israel. The Old Testament account of these events is found in 2 Kings 3:1-27.

The Burnt House of Kathros

The Israeli victory in the Six Days War in 1967 gave them control of the old city of Jerusalem, and this made archaeological work possible in many parts of Jerusalem previously off limits to Israeli scholars. Since '67 they have made many exciting discoveries. One of the most dramatic was the burnt house of Kathros.

In January 1970, Nahman Avigad was excavating in the area where the Upper City had been located in Jesus' day. After clearing away many layers of debris, Avigad found the walls of a house. He dug a trench across one of its rooms to check the strata, and quickly found evidence of intense fire. The limestone used to build the house had changed color as a result of the fire. Black soot and ashes were everywhere.

At that time no archaeological evidence of Jerusalem's destruction by the Romans in 70 A.D. had ever been found, and Avigad began to wonder whether he might have made such a discovery. He found charred wooden beams and evidence that some flammable material, perhaps olive oil, had fed the flames. When excavations reached floor level, he found pottery, broken glass, nails and coins. Most of the coins were from the Jewish revolt against Rome, minted 67-69 A.D. with the inscription, "The Freedom of Zion." These coins were positive archaeological evidence that the house had been burned in the Roman destruction in 70 A.D.

The archaeologists found a spear leaning in the corner of one room. The Roman soldiers may have come so suddenly that whoever put this spear in the corner did not have enough time to pick it up and defend himself. They also found part of the skeleton of a young woman in her early 20s who was killed by the Romans and left on the floor when the house was put to torch. The Upper City, where the burnt house was located, held out for nearly a month after the temple fell. And according to Josephus, when the Romans finally stormed the Upper City, they poured through the streets with swords in hand and "massacred indiscriminately all whom they met, and burnt the houses with all who had taken refuge within." This was exactly what had happened to the young Jewish woman in the burnt house.

Avigad was even able to identify the owners of the house — a prominent priestly family named Kathros. The identification came from a stone weight found in the house with an inscription in Aramaic, "of Bar Kathros." The House of Kathros was already known from a passage in the Talmud: "Woe is me because of the House of Kathros." The families who controlled the Jerusalem priesthood in the first century often abused their office and exploited the people, and the House of Kathros seems to have shared in these corrupt practices.

The burnt house of Kathros was the first tangible evidence that archaeologists had found of Jerusalem's destruction in 70 A.D. (although additional discoveries have been made since 1970). As a result the burnt house stirred deep emotions about Jerusalem's tragic past. In Avigad's words,

> The burning of the Temple and the destruction of Jerusalem — fateful events in the history of the Jewish people — suddenly took on a new and horrible significance. Persons who had previously regarded this catastrophe as stirring but abstract and remote, having occurred two millennia ago, were so visibly moved by the sight that they occasionally would beg permission to take a fistful of soil or a bit of charred wood "in memory of the destruction" (*Biblical Archaeology Review,* Nov./Dec. 1983).

CHAPTER SIX

Herod: the Greatest Builder

Bill Humble:

Herod the Great was the greatest builder in the history of the Bible land. But most of us remember Herod for only one of his deeds, the birth of Jesus and the murder of the babies of Bethlehem. Herod was a very cruel man, and when he ordered the execution of one of his own sons, the emperor Augustus said, "I'd rather be Herod's swine than his son."

But along with his cruelty, Herod was the greatest builder in the history of this land. During the 30 years before Jesus' birth, he built palaces and cities all over the land, and the ruins of many of these buildings are still standing today.

Let's begin here in the old city of Jerusalem. As we have already seen, Herod's crowning achievement was building the temple and the great wall around the temple mountain. Herod was an Idumean in race, but a Jew in religion, so the temple was a sure way for Herod to please his Jewish subjects.

But Herod admired the culture of Greece and Rome, so he built a theater in Jerusalem and a great hippodrome for chariot races. These were offensive to his Jewish subjects.

As for himself, Herod built a great palace on the west side of Jerusalem. He built three tall towers to protect his palace from the north. And he built the fortress of Antonio to guard the temple and keep order.

As Judge Steven Adler explains, the Western Wall of the temple mount is still standing today.

Steven Adler:

The Western Wall is the outer wall of the Second Temple. The exciting thing is that it is the largest area which is still in existence from the time of the Second Temple which stood on the top of the mountain. The large stones are up to 50 or 60 tons in size, and they have borders around the sides, and they were chiseled and brought to this site. The ones at the bottom of the wall are larger than the ones at the top.

Bill Humble:

Recent excavations in the Rabbinic Tunnel near the Western Wall have uncovered a Herodian stone that is 40 feet long and weighs over 400 tons. It's still a mystery how stones of this size could be quarried a half-mile away and moved to this site.

Herod the Great also did vast building work outside Jerusalem, including whole new cities.

We are at Caesarea Maritima, or Caesarea on the Sea, where Herod the Great built one of his most remarkable projects — an artificial harbor, the first time this had ever been done in human history, and along with the harbor, a vast new city. A great amount of archaeological work has been done here in recent years, including underwater archaeology.

The Bible land did not have a good natural harbor, so Herod spent 10 years building an artificial harbor here at Caesarea — an undertaking never before attempted.

Joseph Shulam:

The harbor of Caesarea was the major Roman harbor during the end of the first century B.C. and most of the first century A.D. It was the biggest harbor on the eastern Mediterranean coast. It was built by Herod the Great and the Roman legions that besieged Jerusalem and finally conquered Jerusalem and desecrated the temple in 70 A.D. — most of them at least — landed in the harbor at Caesarea.

Bill Humble:

To create this harbor, Herod built two enormous breakwaters out into the Mediterranean. The south breakwater began here at the present harbor wall and went a third of a mile out into the sea. It was 200 feet wide. To build this breakwater Herod used cut stones, 50 feet long and 18 feet high, and his builders somehow moved them out into the Mediterranean and lowered them down into 120 feet of water.

What made this harbor possible was hydraulic concrete — concrete that will harden under water. The Romans had learned the secret of hydraulic concrete only 25 years earlier, and Herod used it here at Caesarea. Underwater archaeologists recently located a great block of concrete, 50 feet square, that was poured and hardened at the bottom of the sea.

The present small harbor was built by the Crusaders. It lies within Herod's harbor, but the Herodian harbor extended further out into the sea. It was as large as Piraeus, the harbor of Athens, and this made it one of the two or three largest harbors in the Roman world.

When the Crusaders built their harbor, a thousand years after Herod the Great, they used materials from Herodian buildings they tore down. Here are some interesting examples. Archaeologists call this a "secondary use" of earlier materials. And there are still Herodian columns lying in the sea like driftwood.

Herod built a great new city around his harbor with public buildings and temples, warehouses, and piers. Current excavations have uncovered one of those piers. Here is a great stone ring where ships would have been tied up at the pier.

There was a row of large vaulted warehouses behind the piers where the cargoes from the ships could be stored. These have been excavated in recent years. You can see the typical Herodian stones, with margins around the edges, in the walls of these storehouses.

Herod dedicated three of his cities to the emperor Augustus. They were Tiberius, Samaria and Caesarea; and he built temples to Augustus in each of these cities.

Joseph Shulam:

We are here in front of a temple to Augustus that Herod the Great built in honor of the Roman Caesar. Here in Caesarea he had a number of these temples. This one was all lined in marble with three niches, the center of which had a statue of Augustus and was venerated here both by Herod's men and the Roman garrison that was stationed here.

Bill Humble:

Caesarea did not have a natural water supply, so Herod built an aqueduct to bring water from the

Carmel Mountains to the north. There are six miles of these arches, but most of them are still buried under the sand.

However, the aqueduct did not reach all the way to the mountains. Herod cut a tunnel through the limestone, another six miles, to bring the water from the Carmel range to the point where the aqueduct began.

But as we see in one of the arches, there are really two aqueducts side by side. By the second century Caesarea was so large that Herod's aqueduct could not supply the city with water, so the emperor Hadrian had another aqueduct built alongside Herod's. Hadrian's new aqueduct is on the right.

Herod also built a theater at Caesarea, seating 4,000 and facing the Mediterranean Sea. It was excavated in the 1960s by Italian archaeologists, and it has been restored and is used for concerts. Cornelius, the first Gentile Christian, lived here in Caesarea, and as a Roman army officer, he probably came to concerts in this theater.

Here in the theater, the archaeologists found this stone with the inscription, "Pontius Pilate, Prefect of Judaea." You can see the name in Latin, *Pilatus.* This is very important because it is the only extrabiblical evidence of Pilate that has ever been found.

Other important inscriptions have been found at Caesarea. These are Christian inscriptions from the third century. One is covered up with sand to protect it, and we have to clean off the sand before we can see it. We pour a little water on it, and we can read the inscription. It tells Christians, "Don't be afraid of the authorities if you are doing right." And we cover it again with sand.

Nearby there's another round inscription. It's a

verse from Romans 13, admonishing Christians to obey the government.

Caesarea was very important in New Testament history. Philip lived here. Cornelius was converted here. Paul was imprisoned here for two years and set sail from this harbor for Rome. In later Christian history, when the emperor Constantine ordered 50 copies of the Bible made for churches, they were copied here at Caesarea.

The harbor and its city were remarkable feats of ancient building. Perhaps Josephus said it best when he wrote, "At Caesarea, as nowhere else, Herod displayed the grandeur of his character."

Caesarea Philippi is another city that Herod built, and this is not to be confused with Caesarea on the Sea. Caesarea Philippi is located at the base of beautiful Mt. Hermon at the north end of the Bible land. This is where the Jordan River begins in springs flowing out of the base of the mountain. And this is Panias or Banias where the Greeks had a sanctuary to the god Pan back in the days of Alexander the Great.

Caesarea Philippi is mentioned in connection with the ministry of Jesus in Matthew 16, when He and His disciples came here and Peter confessed that He was the Messiah. Excavations are now being conducted here at this ancient Roman site, and archaeologists Vassilios Tzaferis and John Wilson describe these excavations for us.

Vassilios Tzaferis:

We started excavating here two years ago. This is our third season with all the universities from Texas, Los Angeles and Virginia participating, and what we have this year is a nice monument from Herodian times, from the first century A.D. — probably a temple.

Bill Humble:

We know from Josephus that Herod built a temple to the emperor Augustus here at Caesarea Philippi, made of marble, and if this should prove to be that temple, it would be a significant discovery. After Herod the Great built the temple, his son Herod Philip continued building, and this became a major city, named for him and the emperor — Caesar and Philip — Caesarea Philippi.

In 1988 Tzaferis discovered a row of remarkable Herodian arches here.

Vassilios Tzaferis:

We have so far 12 Roman arches built on a straight row, which arches later on were incorporated into another building in the Crusader period. But we believe these arches were part of the forum of the city, the center of the city, where all the monumental and public buildings were found.

John Wilson:

The arches run in a long row. They are intact from floor to ceiling; the ceilings are intact in the arches. They are probably 30 feet deep and 20 to 25 feet high. So they are very large arches, very large rooms, and very unusual that you have them intact from Roman times.

Bill Humble:

Here is a capital from the top of a large column that was found during the '89 season. Look at the size of this capital — more than 3 feet in diameter.

Vassilios Tzaferis:

This is a unique discovery this year, and I believe there is another one found in Masada, not so large as this one, and it dates to the Herodian period in the first century B.C.

Row of first-century arches discovered at Caesarea Philippi in 1988.

Bill Humble:

The digging will continue here at Caesarea Philippi for several years, and this promises to be one of the most exciting excavations anywhere in Israel.

We have now come to Samaria and to the Roman forum that Herod built here. Samaria had been the capital of the northern kingdom 'til the Assyrians destroyed it in 721 B.C. Herod rebuilt the city on a grand scale and named it Sebaste, the Greek name of the emperor Augustus.

This forum was the heart of the Herodian city. The columns were part of a portico around the forum, like the porticos around the temple in Jerusalem.

Herod also built a temple here at Samaria, another pagan temple to Augustus. The platform where the temple stood and the steps leading up to it are still here. This temple to Augustus, like the one at Caesarea, shows that Herod was torn between conflicting loyalties. In Jerusalem he was a Jew, and he rebuilt the temple to the God of Israel. But in Samaria and Caesarea, he was a Roman pagan and built temples to the god Augustus.

Along with the temples to the gods, Herod built palaces for himself — at Jerusalem, at Masada, and at Jericho.

Joseph Shulam:

One of Herod's greatest palaces was right here in Jericho. It was his winter palace that was built from bricks with plaster and stucco that he often painted. Even the columns were fluted with plaster.

Bill Humble:

This was unusual construction for Herod — brick instead of stone. Here is a circular bath with brick walls around it, and here are columns made of bricks. These walls and columns would have been plastered and painted to look like marble, like this column. And here is a column fluted with plaster.

Why a winter palace at Jericho?

Joseph Shulam:

It is warm in the winter even though 15 miles from here in Jerusalem it might be a snow blizzard.

Bill Humble:

During the winter Herod entertained Roman dignitaries here when they came through the Bible land. This was a large palace covering three acres with buildings and courtyards, gardens and fountains.

As a Jew, Herod practiced the ceremonial washings required by the purity laws, so every palace had to have *mikvoth,* or baptistries.

Joseph Shulam:

Here in Jericho Herod had a number of *mikvoth* with a water system that flowed from one into another in order to preserve the water flowing while people were taking their ritual baths. The ritual baths were taken for preservation and keeping of the Old Testament purity laws.

Bill Humble:

A hundred years earlier, the Maccabean kings had had a winter palace here, and Herod incorporated some of those Maccabean buildings in his palace.

Joseph Shulam:

Herod the Great died here in this palace, and after his death, his body was carried to Herodium, another of his great palaces, and there he was buried. In Herodium archaeologists have recently been excavating and looking for his tomb, but the precise spot of his tomb has not yet been discovered.

Bill Humble:

Even though Herod the Great was the greatest builder in the history of this land, we don't know what he looked like. Archaeologists have found no bust of Herod, not even a coin with his inscription on it. But after building cities like Jerusalem and

Caesarea on the Sea, when Herod died in 4 B.C., he had left an imprint on this land that 2,000 years could not erase.

Scriptures for Study

Acts 8:40. Philip's preaching at Caesarea.
Acts 10:1-48. Conversion of Cornelius.
Acts 18:22,23; 21:7-16. Paul's visits to Caesarea.
Acts 23:12–26:32. Paul's imprisonment at Caesarea.
Matthew 16:13-20. Jesus' promise at Caesarea Philippi.

Notes from Archaeology

Herod the Great

Herod the Great is usually remembered for only one event that happened near the end of his 33-year reign as king of the Jews: the birth of Jesus and the cruel order to murder the male children around Bethlehem. Herod was often guilty of such cruelty. But what many do not know is that, along with his cruelty, Herod was one of the ablest rulers in the Roman Empire and the most tireless builder the Bible land has ever known.

Herod was an Idumean or Edomite in race, a Jew in religion (for John Hyrcanus had forced all Idumeans to be circumcised and become Jews a century earlier), and a Graeco-Roman in cultural and political ties. The Romans had made Herod's father, Antipater, the procurator of Judaea. Herod was a shrewd opportunist, and in the turmoil in Rome that followed the assassination of Julius Caesar, Herod went to Rome. And with the support of Mark Antony and Octavian, he persuaded the Roman Senate to proclaim him the King of Judaea. Herod returned to Judaea, and with Roman army support, he defeated the Parthians, captured Jerusalem, and began his reign in 37 B.C.

Herod's reign is often divided into three periods:

(1) *Consolidation of power* (37-25 B.C.). It took a decade for Herod to consolidate his power, deprive the Jewish Sanhedrin of its political influence, and get rid of the Maccabean princes who might threaten his reign. Herod married Mariamne, a beautiful Maccabean princess. He loved her madly, but when she was accused of unfaithfulness, he had her executed, then almost went insane over what he had done. Josephus reports that Herod wandered around his palace calling for Mariamne and ordering his servants to bring her to him. Mariamne's brother, Aristobulus, was drowned in a "playful" scuffle in Herod's swimming pool at Jericho. Herod was accused of his murder but cleared himself in a meeting with Mark Antony.

(2) *Prosperity* (25-13 B.C.). The middle years of Herod's reign brought peace, prosperity and remarkable building projects throughout the land. He built public buildings, hippodromes, gymnasiums, public baths, palaces, fortresses, temples, and even new cities all over the land. He built an artificial harbor at Caesarea on the Sea, the first time this had ever been done, and a magnificent new city around the harbor. Herod rebuilt the Second Temple in Jerusalem and enlarged the temple mount on which it stood. The result was so striking that the rabbis said, "One who has not seen Herod's temple has never seen a beautiful building."

Today, impressive remains of Herodian buildings can still be seen all over the Bible land: the temple mount in Jerusalem, the Tomb of the Patriarchs in Hebron, Herodium, Masada, Machaerus, Samaria, Caesarea on the Sea, Caesarea Philippi, and the winter palace at Jericho. It seems almost impossible that King Herod, ruling over a small Roman province, could have had so many great building projects within a span of 15 years, but somehow he did.

Nor were Herod's building activities limited to the Bible land. Herod also carried on vast building outside his kingdom — the Temple of Apollo at Rhodes, public buildings at Nicopolis, Antioch, Tyre, Sidon and Damascus. He endowed the Olympic Games and served as president of the games when he was on a visit to Rome in 12 B.C.

(3) *Family Turmoil* (13-4 B.C.). The last 10 years of Herod's life were filled with such family turmoil and intrigue that Josephus has described it as a time of "domestic civil war." Herod had 10 wives and at least 15 children. With that many sons aspiring to the throne, it is no wonder that the family was in turmoil. Josephus has reported that Herod's court was a scene of distrust and intrigue — suspects were tortured and killed, spies were everywhere, and Herod's sons accused one another of plotting the murder of their father.

After Herod executed his beloved Mariamne, he favored the two sons she had borne him, Alexander and Aristobulus. He sent them to Rome for the finest education and journeyed to Rome to accompany them home to Jerusalem. But when their brothers accused them of plotting against their father, Herod became suspicious and finally ordered that they be killed by strangulation at Samaria, where he had married their mother, Mariamne, 30 years earlier. They were buried in the tomb of their Maccabean forebearers in the mountaintop fortress Alexandrium. The Emperor Augustus is reported to have said, "I had rather be Herod's swine than his son."

Herod's winter palace in Jericho where he died.

Herod's eldest son, Antipater, was scheduled to succeed him, but when the dying Herod learned that Antipater was trying to seize the throne, he ordered his execution. Five days later, Herod died. As he neared death, Herod realized there would be little sorrow in the land at his passing. So he ordered important Jews from all over the land brought to Jericho and held in the hippodrome, with orders that they be killed at his death so that the land would be filled with mourning. Thankfully, the order was not carried out.

After living through 10 years of such bloody turmoil in his own family, and now an old man, sullen, suspicious, and dying from an awful disease, Herod probably felt few pangs of conscience when he gave the order, "Kill all the baby boys around Bethlehem."

Herod died at his winter palace at Jericho and was borne across the Judaean desert to another palace, Herodium, where he was buried in a coffin of solid gold. At that time Herodium was the largest palace that had ever been built anywhere in the Roman world. Located four miles southeast of Bethlehem, Herodium looms as a symbol of the strange extremes in Herod's character. A remarkable builder whose forts and palaces still stand as 2,000-year-old monuments to his greatness, Herod was capable of heartless cruelty, and it mattered little whether the victims were nameless boys at Bethlehem or his own sons.

The Harbor at Caesarea

One of Herod's most remarkable building projects was his artificial harbor at Caesarea on the Sea — the first such man-made harbor ever constructed — a harbor that both Peter and Paul visited. Peter came to Caesarea to open the door of Christ's church to Gentiles. As Paul returned to Jerusalem at the end of his second missionary journey, his ship landed at Caesarea. Once again, at the end of the third journey, he landed at Caesarea and spent some time in the home of the evangelist Philip before going up to Jerusalem. Later, when the Romans learned about a plot against Paul's life (Acts 23), he was escorted to Caesarea for his own safety, remained imprisoned there for two years, and then sailed from Caesarea to Rome.

Whenever Paul came to Caesarea, he was probably amazed at the size of the man-made harbor and the magnificence of the new city around it. According to Josephus the harbor was as large as Pireas, the port of Athens, and thus was one of the two or three largest harbors in the Roman world.

The harbor entrance was on the northwest to shelter it from fierce Mediterranean storms that blew in from the southwest. As Paul's ship approached the harbor entrance, he would have seen two enormous breakwaters enclosing the harbor. Standing in front of the breakwaters on either side of the harbor mouth, there were large pillars rising up out of the sea with three large statues on each pillar. The statues would have been a welcome and awesome sight to weary travelers after a long Mediterranean crossing.

The two great breakwaters that encircled the harbor were remarkable feats of ancient building. The south breakwater was more than 200 feet wide and extended one-third of a mile out into the sea, then curved northward to the harbor entrance. The north breakwater extended about 800 feet out into the Mediterranean. The harbor entrance was on the northwest, 60 feet wide, with the statues welcoming ships inside. According to Josephus, the blocks of stone used to build the breakwaters were 50 feet long, 18 feet wide, and 10 feet high. Somehow, these enormous blocks of stone were carried a third of a mile out into the Mediterranean and lowered into 120 feet of water. Even with modern cranes, it would be a formidable undertaking, so we can only wonder how Herod's engineers were able to do it. Just a few years earlier, Roman engineers had discovered hydraulic concrete (concrete that will harden under water), and without this technology, Caesarea would have been impossible. Herod's engineers poured large blocks of concrete (40 by 50 feet) onto the ocean floor, and the enormous blocks of stone were lowered down onto this concrete foundation. The ruins of these great breakwaters, now entirely under water, can still be seen in aerial photographs of the Caesarea harbor.

Inside the harbor were piers where the ships anchored and large warehouses where the cargoes were unloaded and stored. It is obvious that much of the commerce of the eastern Mediterranean passed through Caesarea.

The new city that Herod built at Caesarea matched the magnificence of the harbor. Much of the city was built of imported white marble, and had a temple in honor of the Emperor Augustus, a hippodrome seating 38,000, a theater (now restored and used for concerts), and a subterranean sewer system that was flushed by Mediterranean tides.

Caesarea had no natural water supply, so Herod built an aqueduct and tunnel to bring water from the Carmel Mountains into the city. The aqueduct was supported by a line of tall arches six-and-a-half miles long. (Actually, there were two aqueducts, for the Emperor Hadrian built a second-century aqueduct that parallels the Herodian aqueduct, arch for arch.) These aqueducts are now buried under the sand, but the arches near Caesarea have been uncovered. The aqueduct connected with a tunnel that carried water from the Carmel Mountains to the point where the aqueduct began. The tunnel was cut through the limestone hills and is six miles long and about 4 feet high. The combined length of Herod's tunnel and aqueduct was 13½ miles.

Underwater Archaeology

Underwater archaeology is something new in our exploration of the past, and Caesarea is the one biblical site where it has already been very valuable. (Texas A & M University is a leader in underwater archaeology, but their work has been with sunken ancient ships of the Turkish coast and elsewhere.)

The first underwater archaeology at Caesarea was in 1960 when the Link Expedition for Underwater Archaeology used divers to explore the large breakwaters that enclosed Herod's harbor. The divers were able to determine that the Herodian harbor was about three-and-a-half acres in size. The Link Expedition also developed equipment for sifting the ocean-bed sand within the harbor to recover artifacts from the bottom of the sea. The most important artifact recovered was very small, a coin or medal about the size of a dime. The coin pictured the entrance to a harbor, probably Caesarea. Two letters, KA, were found on the coin, which may be an abbreviation for Caesarea. The coin shows towers with statues on either side of the harbor mouth, just as Josephus has described them.

Additional underwater work was done at Caesarea in 1982 when scuba divers for the Caesarea Ancient Harbor Excavation Project found parts of a wooden form where concrete blocks had been poured at the bottom of the sea. The wooden beams and forms had been covered with sand and silt, and this kept them from rotting away.

We know that Roman engineers had discovered the secret of hydraulic concrete (concrete that will harden beneath the sea) only a few years before Herod built Caesarea. The famous work *On Architecture* by Vitruvius was published in 25 B.C., and it describes a special sand called *pozzolana* that would cause concrete to harden under water. Vitruvius wrote, "There is also a kind of powder . . . found in the country belonging to the towns about Mt. Vesuvius. This substance, when mixed with lime and rubble, not only lends strength to buildings of other kinds, but even when piers of it are constructed in the sea, they set hard under water."

Herod's builders had learned of this work, and it was hydraulic concrete that made the Caesarea harbor possible. The scuba divers who explored the harbor in 1982 found two great blocks of concrete that had been poured at the bottom of the sea. The larger block measures approximately 40 by 50 feet, is intact to a height of 5 feet, and contains 10,000 cubic feet of concrete. The second block still has fragments of the wooden form around it.

These two blocks of concrete are located just outside the harbor entrance, but they are not part of the breakwaters that enclosed the harbor. So the archaeologists have concluded that these blocks were foundations for the towers that stood on either side of the harbor with the large statues on them (as described in Josephus). Unfortunately, the underwater archaeologists failed to find any remains of the statues.

Herod's Income

How was Herod able to finance so many great building projects? Not just Caesarea — for he was building at Jerusalem, Masada, Herodium, Samaria, and at cities outside his realm. Herod probably taxed all his subjects heavily, but with a population of perhaps four million, mostly poor farmers, their taxes could hardly have produced the vast sums that Herod spent on his building projects.

One discovery at Caesarea may help to answer the question of how Herod financed his building. Just east of the harbor, archaeologists found a large vaulted room. Built of sandstone blocks with the typical Herodian margin around them, the room was 96 feet long and 15 feet high. The room was so large that it took two years to excavate the debris and show that the room had served as a warehouse for the harbor. When archaeologists got to the floor level, they found huge quantities of broken pottery. It was from typical first-century pottery jars (amphorae) that were brought into the Bible land from Italy, Spain and Gaul. Some amphora handles had stamps telling what they had contained. The excavators also found coins from the reign of Nero (54-68 A.D.) that had been minted at Caesarea.

After the first vaulted room was excavated, the archaeologists found the outlines of others beside it. They are so large and so filled with debris that they have not been excavated. But it is estimated that there may be as many as 20 of these vaulted warehouses in a large block, and there may be as many as five more blocks of warehouses around the harbor.

These warehouses are evidence that the Caesarea harbor was the hub of vast commerce that connected the eastern Mediterranean with such distant lands as Italy, Spain and Gaul to the west, and Arabia to the east. The income from this commerce would have been enormous and may explain how Herod the Great found the revenue to finance his widespread building program.

There is a hint of Herod's great wealth in one provision in his will — a gift of 10 million pieces of silver to his patron, the Emperor Augustus.

Chapter Seven

Herod the Great's Palaces

Bill Humble:

Herod the Great was a remarkable man, the greatest builder in the history of this Bible land. He rebuilt Jerusalem and made it a Graeco-Roman city. He rebuilt the temple, and when Jesus taught in the temple, it was Herod's temple. He built a new seaport, Caesarea on the Sea, where the apostle Paul was imprisoned for two years.

But along with these new cities, Herod also built palaces and fortresses for himself all over the land. The most spectacular was at Masada.

Masada is a great mountaintop fortress overlooking the western shore of the Dead Sea, and this is the most awesome of all the building projects of Herod the Great. This mountain of rock is 1,300 feet high, and it looks like a ship sailing through the sands of the Judean desert.

Herod knew about Masada long before he built his fortress here. Before he became king, he had been forced to flee to Rome. And he left his mother and Mariamne here on Masada. Mariamne was the Maccabean princess he would marry.

Later when he wanted to build a palace-fortress that could withstand any siege, he chose Masada as the site. The summit is surprisingly flat and 1,900 feet long. It must have taken an army of workers to do all this building, and in the summer, the temperature climbs to 130 degrees here in the desert.

After Herod's death, Masada was an outpost of the Roman army. Then in 70 A.D. Jewish Zealots seized Masada, and three years later their last stand became one of the most heroic moments in all Jewish history.

Herod built a double wall (archaeologists call this a "casemate" wall) all the way around the edge of the summit. This meant that if an attacking army managed to scale the cliffs, they still faced a double defensive wall. There were 37 towers in the wall. Herod made sure that no army could mount a successful attack against Masada.

Across the wall we look down to the Dead Sea 1,300 feet below and to Moab over on the east side of the sea.

Herod had two palaces on Masada. One was a large western palace. The other was an amazing, three-level palace clinging to the north end of Masada. From the top we look down to the middle level, where the circular foundations remain, and to the lowest level further down.

From the side we can see how the palace clings to the mountainside — a remarkable feat of ancient building. The Israeli army engineers have installed a steel stairway, and this makes it possible for visitors to see all the palace.

We are now on the lowest level of Herod the Great's three-level palace. It's 105 feet from the highest level up there down to this level. It is decorated with beautiful columns and frescoes on the wall. Josephus knew about this palace and described it in his *Antiquities,* but people doubted the accuracy of it 'til the excavations were done here. Now we know it's just exactly like Josephus described it. It must have been Herod the Great's private retreat.

The walls between the columns are plastered and painted to resemble marble, and they still look like marble after 2,000 years.

Why was this palace built here? To catch the cool breezes that nearly always blow across the north end of Masada.

Near the palace on the summit, there are large storage rooms. Many of them have been excavated and restored, but some have not. When the Zealots seized Masada, these rooms were filled with Roman weapons and food, and this is how they were able to hold out for three years.

Masada also had a synagogue built into the outer wall. It's important because it is one of the two oldest synagogues ever discovered. It was in use as a synagogue while the temple was still standing in Jerusalem.

Archaeologists found a number of biblical manuscripts on Masada, and some were buried here in the synagogue in a little chamber called a *genizah.*

It is interesting that another manuscript found on Masada is one of the Essene documents from Qumran, and this shows that there may have been some Essenes among the Zealots at Masada.

Palaces have to have baths, and these are the pillars in a Roman caldarium, or hot bath. And these are some of the beautiful mosaics from the palaces and baths. Notice the black restoration line on the walls. This shows where the ancient walls were still standing intact, but above the line they have put the stones back in place.

Herod had an outdoor bathing pool with broad plastered steps down into the water. He even had a larger swimming pool — all the comforts of Jerusalem here in the desert.

What about a water supply for this great fortress? The rainfall in this part of Israel is no more than 2 or 3 inches per year. But the engineers of Herod the Great had built a series of dams around the base to trap the water. They carried the water to the summit by slaves or animals and deposited the water in a number of cisterns here on the summit. These are the steps going down into the largest of the cisterns. It holds more than a million gallons of water.

Herod lived in a world without cable cars, so how did he and his family get up to their palaces? They climbed. There was a steep path on the Dead Sea side that led up to the top. Josephus knew about this path, and he says that it was called the "snake path" because of its "continual windings." It was so steep and narrow that a handful of men on the summit could hold off an army.

Archaeologists have found this snake path, and today it's a strenuous 40-minute climb up to the top. Herod may have ridden a horse or sure-footed donkey up the snake path.

Today Masada is a national shrine to the people of Israel, and this is because of the Zealots' last stand here in the year 73 A.D. When Jerusalem was destroyed in 70 A.D., a band of Zealots seized Masada, Josephus says, "by treachery." There were 960 of them — men, women and children — under the leadership of Eleazar ben Yair. Safe here in Herod's fortress, they defied the Romans until the spring of 73 A.D.

Then General Flavius Silva, the procurator of Judaea, brought an army of 5,000 men and laid siege to Masada. They built a siege wall and army camps around the base so that none of the Zealots could escape. From the summit, we can see one of those camps with the siege wall below it.

But how could anyone attack Masada? No army could scale those 1,300 feet high cliffs.

General Silva's strategy was to use Jewish slaves and build a great siege ramp up to the summit. Look at the size of that ramp. No telling how many slaves died here as they toiled in the desert sun.

When the ramp was finished, the Romans moved their war machines up the ramp — a siege tower and battering ram — and they knocked a gaping hole in the casemate wall.

That night Eleazar called his men together — here in the synagogue. They all knew that they would be overwhelmed the next day, and Eleazar pleaded that death would be better than crucifixion, rape and slavery. They set the buildings on fire, then each man bade his wife and children a tearful farewell and killed them with his own sword. Archaeologists found the sandals and braided hair of one of those Zealot wives.

Next, 10 of the Zealots killed all of their comrades, and then they chose lots to see which one would kill the other nine, then fall on his own sword.

The archaeologists may have found those lots in this room — pieces of broken pottery with a name on each one. One name is ben Yair, their leader.

The next morning when the Romans stormed up the ramp, instead of the desperate fighting they expected, they found the bodies of 960 Zealots who had chosen death rather than slavery. Josephus says that the Romans stood in awe at such courage.

When Yigael Yadin excavated Masada in the 1960s, he found the remains of some of the Zealots, including the women, and these were buried in a memorial mound at the base of the Roman ramp.

Joseph Shulam, an Israeli who lives in Jerusalem, explains what Masada means to him.

Joseph Shulam:

As an Israeli, I feel that Masada is important for two main reasons. One is the great tenacity of the Zealot warriors in Masada for freedom and for the desire not to be captive to Rome. And, of course, the second thing, it reminds me as a Jewish Christian that the temple was destroyed and we lost the battle because of our sins. As Eleazar ben Yair, the captain of the Zealot forces at Masada, said in his last speech that is recorded by Josephus, that Jerusalem fell because of our sins. So Masada has a dual message. One is a message of valor and bravery. The other is a message that sin always brings a calamity.

Bill Humble:

Masada is a symbol of the national spirit and patriotism in Israel today. It is the Alamo of the ancient world and far more to the people of Israel. There are certain elite units of the Israeli army that come to Masada at night, take their oath of induction into the Israeli army, and make the vow, "Masada will never fall again."

Joseph Shulam:

Masada is a reminder to every Israeli and every Jew that you don't have to give up.

Bill Humble:

Herod must have felt a sense of security in mountaintop fortresses. The Maccabean kings had built the fortress Alexandrium on a mountain 18 miles north of Jericho. Herod restored this fortress in 38 B.C. to guard the Jordan valley. When Herod executed the two sons of Mariamne, the Jewish wife he loved so dearly, he had them buried here at Alexandrium in the tomb of their Maccabean ancestors.

Herodium is another of the great palaces built by Herod the Great. Herodium is located about three miles east of Bethlehem.

Herodium was also built on a mountain, and even though it looks like an extinct volcano, it's a natural hill, and atop this hill Herod built a circular palace seven stories high. This is the only palace that Herod named for himself.

It has two circular walls, which we can see here, nearly 40 feet apart and with rooms built in the space between the walls. Inside, there is a large open area 200 feet in diameter. It's about like a modern hotel, built in a circle, with all the rooms looking down into the atrium.

Today when we stand on the walls and look down into that atrium, it seems, again, that we're looking down into a volcano crater. The main living area of the palace was located down in the atrium.

On the east side there was a large courtyard that was decorated with columns and fountains and gardens. Many of these columns are still standing today. In Herod's day it must have looked like a beautiful garden sunk in the heart of a mountain.

On the opposite side there were the family quarters and baths. Herod had a complete Roman-style bath with hot and cold rooms. The beehive architecture here in the bath is very interesting. Notice how the keystones hold the dome together. The royal tombs at Mycene in Greece, from the 12th century B.C., have this beehive architecture, and Herod's builders copied it here.

Herodium.

Herodium also had a synagogue. This synagogue and the one at Masada are the two oldest synagogues ever discovered. Notice the stone seats around the walls — just like the one at Masada.

Herod built four large towers in the outer wall of this palace. Three of them are semi-circular and extend out from the wall. But the one on the east is a full circle, 55 feet in diameter, and is solid masonry all the way through.

Herodium was both a palace and a fortress, so it is not surprising to find these catapult stones piled here.

After the palace was finished, Herod piled earth and stone up around the lower stories, and it is only these lower stories below ground that have survived.

But there is more to Herodium than the mountaintop palace which archaeologists call Upper Herodium. Lower Herodium is at the base of the mountain, and there's another palace down there that is 400 feet long. The foundations of this building can still be seen, but not much more.

Lower Herodium also had a large pool 210 feet long and 9 feet deep. The stone walls are 5 feet thick and plastered to keep the water from leaking out. There was an island in the middle of the pool with a circular building and columns on the island. This pool was probably used for swimming and boating, and it also served as an architectural focus for Herodium. An aqueduct three miles long brought water to the pool.

The complex of buildings at Herodium covered about 45 acres, and this made it the largest palace in the empire. Later, Nero would build a larger palace at Rome, but at the time, Herodium was the biggest palace anywhere in the Roman empire.

Herodium is never mentioned in the New Testament. But it was a familiar sight to all who traveled around Bethlehem. When Jesus crossed the Mount of Olives from Bethany to Jerusalem, there was Herodium sticking up on the horizon.

An intriguing archaeological puzzle here at Herodium is the location of Herod's tomb.

Joseph Shulam:

Herod died here in this palace in Jericho, and after his death, his body was carried to Herodium for burial.

Bill Humble:

Josephus tells about Herod's death at his winter palace in Jericho. And he tells how the body was placed in a coffin of solid gold and carried in a funeral procession from Jericho across the Judean desert to Herodium for burial. An Israeli archaeologist, Ehud Netzer, has spent the last decade searching for Herod's tomb, but to no avail.

Some scholars think that Herod's tomb is hidden somewhere in the massive east tower, but Netzer does not agree with this. The Jews never buried the dead in a building where they lived. Tombs were always outside the city.

Netzer discovered a large monumental building between the pool and the base of the mountain. This building has the finest stone work, and Netzer thought this would prove to be the entrance to Herod's tomb cut into the side of the mountain. But Netzer found no tomb.

Most scholars think that if Herod's tomb is ever found, it will be empty, looted long ago in antiquity. But there is the intriguing possibility, however slight, that the tomb might be found undisturbed, with gold to rival King Tut's tomb in Egypt.

When Herod the Great was buried here at Herodium, there was little mourning in the land. Herod was an Edomite, not a Jew, in race. And the Graeco-Roman culture he loved and admired was anathema to the Jews. But Herod the Great left a legacy that would never disappear from this land: new cities and palaces all over the land, many of them still standing today.

If Herod's tomb is ever discovered, the epitaph should read, "Herod — the greatest builder this land has ever known."

Scriptures for Study

The New Testament never mentions Masada or

Herodium. But the New Testament does have information about Herod the Great:

Matthew 2:1-18. Herod the Great, the wise men, and the death of the children of Bethlehem.

Matthew 2:19-23. Herod's death.

Notes from Archaeology

Excavating Masada

Herod's mountaintop palace-fortress, Masada, is the most awesome archaeological site anywhere in the Bible land, and the work of excavating it in the 1960s was the most challenging, perhaps awesome, archaeological work undertaken in Israel. Yigael Yadin directed the excavations. In his book, *Masada,* that followed the excavations, he wrote that it had been the dream of every Israeli archaeologist to excavate Masada. There was not another ancient site quite like it, and because of the Zealots' last stand there in 73 A.D., Masada was a deeply moving symbol of courage to all Israelis.

Yadin recruited hundreds of volunteers for the work on Masada, and with the support of the Israeli Army Corps of Engineers, he was able to complete the excavations in two seasons, October through May in 1963-64, and November through April in 1964-65. Normally, the work on such a large site would have required a decade or longer. The desert heat around Masada is almost unbearable in July and August, with temperatures climbing to 130 or 140, so Yadin did not work in the summers. Soon after Yadin finished the excavations, Masada was opened to the public as a national park.

What made Masada such a challenge was the lack of roads, water and electricity around the site. Today, there is a cable car that carries tourists to the summit, but in the 1960s there were only two ways to get to the top. One was the "snake path." This was the ancient route used in Herod's time. It is on the east side facing the Dead Sea and is so steep and winding that, according to Josephus, it was called the "snake path." The other route to the summit was on the west, up the ramp that the Romans built in 73 A.D. Yadin had to decide whether to establish his tent-camp where workers would live at the base of the snake path or ramp. He chose the western (Roman ramp) side for the camp, since the snake path would have entailed a strenuous 50-minute climb for everyone working on the summit.

Masada.

The Israeli Corps of Engineers built a road to the camp, but it was so rough that it required four-wheel-drive vehicles to bring in the volunteers and supplies. And there were times when the road washed out, and the camp had to be supplied by helicopter. Electricity was supplied by generators brought to the site. Water was a much greater problem until they discovered an abandoned pipeline about four miles away and used it to bring water to the camp.

Many volunteers would be needed to work on Masada, but Yadin knew there was widespread interest in it. He put a brief announcement in Israeli newspapers and in the London *Observer*, and these resulted in thousands of inquiries from 28 countries from people who wanted to take part in the excavations. The volunteers who were accepted had to pay their own airfare to Israel, had to agree to work for a minimum of two weeks, and had to live in tents with 10 beds to the tent. But thousands came, and during the 46 weeks of digging, the work force averaged 300 at all times.

The work days were strenuous with the workers hiking up the Roman ramp at dawn and working, often in hotter weather than they were accustomed to, until mid-afternoon. Even so, the long dreary evenings became a problem. The volunteers organized nightly entertainment, performed in many languages, and representing diverse cultures. One of the volunteers remarked that there was probably nowhere else on earth where such a heterogeneous group could sit together with such primitive accommodations and enjoy such diverse entertainment.

Working on an archaeological site is always hard, dirty work, sometimes with little excitement or rewarding discoveries. But the volunteers who came from around the world to work at Masada all knew the dramatic story of the Zealots' last stand and death, and occasionally, there were moments of high drama when they uncovered artifacts that had belonged to the Zealots. According to Yadin, the greatest moment came when they entered a Zealot room and found, under a layer of ashes, the charred sandals of small children and broken cosmetic vessels. He recalled, "We could sense the very atmosphere of their last tragic hour."

Today there is no other archaeological site in Israel that is quite as awesome as Masada. It is a little unfortunate that tourists go to Masada in air-conditioned buses, ride to the summit in cable cars, look at some of the Herodian buildings, and then hurry back down before the day gets too hot. They can have little feeling for the hardships of Zealot family life on Masada. Nor can they share either the excitement or the hardships of the thousands of volunteers whose work opened Masada for their brief tourist visit.

Yigael Yadin's book, *Masada,* is an exciting account of the excavations. It is written in a popular style, has many beautiful color illustrations, and is highly recommended for anyone interested in archaeology.

Josephus and the Zealots

Before the excavations at Masada, our only source of information about Herod's fortress and the Zealots' last stand there in 73 A.D. was the Jewish historian Josephus. Josephus lived through the Jewish war against the Romans and was involved in the fighting. When it began in 66 A.D., he was a commander at Jotapata in Galilee. The city fell after a 47-day siege, and Josephus and other survivors hid in a cave under the city. They vowed death rather than submission, and they all, except Josephus and one other, killed themselves. Josephus later went over to the Roman side. When Jerusalem lay under siege, he was with the Roman armies, pleading with his people to surrender Jerusalem so that the city and temple would be spared from destruction.

Despite his pro-Roman sympathies, Josephus has left a detailed and sympathetic account of the Zealots' last stand. His account tells of General Flavius Silva's siege, the siege wall and camps built around the base of the mountain, the building of the assault ramp, and the use of siege tower and battering ram to make a breach in the casemate wall at the top of the ramp. Josephus tells how the Zealots tried to throw up a new inner wall of timber and earth. But when they set fire to the Romans' battering ram, the wind suddenly shifted and their wooden wall caught fire and went up in flames.

Now defenseless, the Zealots knew that they would be overwhelmed the next morning. Josephus tells how Eleazar called his bravest men together in the synagogue that night and called on them to accept death rather than torture, crucifixion and rape at the hands of the Romans. Josephus has preserved Eleazar's speech, and here is part of what he said to his men:

> Since we, long ago, my generous friends, resolved never to be servants to the Romans, nor to any other than to God himself, who alone is the true and just Lord of mankind, the time is now come that obliges us to make that resolution true in practice.
>
> We were the very first that revolted against them, and we are the last that fight against them; and I cannot but esteem it a favour that God has granted us, that it is still in our power to die bravely, and in a state of freedom, which hath not been the case with others who were conquered unexpectedly. It is very plain that we shall be taken within a day's time;

> but it is still an eligible thing to die after a glorious manner together with our dearest friends. This is what our enemies themselves cannot by any means hinder, although they be very desirous to take us alive.
>
> We are openly deprived by God himself of all hope of deliverance; for that fire which was driven upon our enemies did not, of its own accord, turn back upon the wall which we had built: this was the effect of God's anger against us for our manifold sins, which we have been guilty of in a most insolent and extravagant manner with regard to our own countrymen; the punishments of which let us not receive from the Romans but from God himself, as executed by our own hands, for these will be more moderate rather than the other.
>
> Let our wives die before they are abused, and our children before they have tasted of slavery; and after we have slain them, let us bestow that glorious benefit upon one another mutually. . . .
>
> But first let us destroy our money and the fortress by fire; for I am well assured that this will be a great grief to the Romans, that they shall not be able to seize upon our bodies, and shall fail of our wealth also; and let us spare nothing but our provisions; for they will be a testimonial when we are dead that we were not subdued for want of necessaries; but that, according to our original resolution, we have preferred death before slavery.

According to Josephus, the Zealot fighters agreed to their leader's grim plea. After setting fire to the fortress, the men embraced their wives and children with the longest parting kisses and then killed them. Josephus says that every man took part in this "terrible execution" and killed his own dearest ones. Next, the men chose 10 of their number to become the executioners. All the others threw themselves on the ground with their arms around their lifeless loved ones and waited for the blows to fall. Finally, the last 10 cast lots to see which one would kill his nine comrades, then fall on his own sword.

When the Romans mounted their final assault the next morning, instead of fighting there was a "terrible solitude" and the bodies of 960 soldiers, wives and children who had chosen death's freedom rather than Roman slavery. Josephus says the Romans found no pleasure in the grim scene, even though it was their enemies. "Nor could they do other than wonder at the courage of their resolution, and at the immovable contempt of death which so great a number of them had shown."

How could Josephus write such a detailed and moving account of the Zealots' death? Where did he get his information? How could he report Eleazar's words to his men?

When the Roman troops fanned out across the summit, they discovered two elderly women (one a relative of Eleazar) and five children still alive. They had hidden in one of the underground cisterns on Masada and were overlooked as the Zealots killed one another. We do not know whether Josephus interviewed the two women or heard their story from the Roman soldiers. But there can be little doubt that his dramatic account was based on their testimony.

Before the Masada excavations, Josephus' account of the Zealots seemed so unbelievable that many scholars were skeptical of his credibility. But according to Yadin, the excavations verified Josephus at so many points, both in descriptions of the Herodian buildings and details of the Zealots' stand, that scholars now treat Josephus with greater respect.

Herod's Burial at Herodium

Josephus is an invaluable source of information about Herod the Great. Without Josephus, many important facts about Herod's reign, including his burial at Herodium, would be unknown. Here is Josephus' account of Herod's funeral and burial:

> The king's funeral next occupied attention. Archelaus, omitting nothing that could contribute to its magnificence, brought forth all the royal ornaments to accompany the procession in honour of the deceased. The bier was of solid gold, studded with precious stones, and had a covering of purple, embroidered with various colors; on this lay the body enveloped in a purple robe, a diadem encircling the head and surmounted by a crown of gold, the sceptre beside his right hand. Around the bier were Herod's sons and a large group of his relations; these were followed by the guards, the Thracian contingent, Germans and Gauls, all equipped as for war. The remainder of the troops marched in front, armed and in orderly array, led by their commanders and subordinate officers; behind these came five hundred of Herod's servants and freedmen, carrying spices. The body was thus conveyed for a distance of two hundred furlongs to Herodium, where, in accordance with the directions of the deceased, it was interred. So ended Herod's reign.

When Ehud Netzer wrote a doctoral dissertation under Yigael Yadin (excavator of Masada) in 1972, his subject was Herodium. Netzer has been working at Herodium ever since and has excavated many parts of Upper Herodium. Recently, he has cleared out a maze of tunnels that honeycomb the mountain and were used by Jewish rebels during the Bar Kochba Revolt in 135 A.D. Safely hidden in these tunnels, the rebels slipped out at night to attack Romans positions. Netzer also excavated the 210-foot-long pool at the base of the mountain. But unfortunately, the real goal of Netzer's work — Herod's tomb — has eluded him.

Herod's tomb may never be found. Even if it is, Netzer knows that it was probably looted in antiquity. But students of the New Testament have to be intrigued by the possibility, albeit slight, that Herod's tomb might someday be found undisturbed. And when we remember the hoard of gold artifacts found in King Tutankhamen's tomb in Egypt in 1922, we can only imagine what magnificent treasures might be found in Herod's tomb alongside the solid gold coffin studded with jewels.

CHAPTER EIGHT

Athens and Corinth

Bill Humble:

This is Mars' Hill in Athens where Paul came on his second missionary journey and where he preached the remarkable sermon about the unknown god, found in Acts 17. This must have been one of the most dramatic moments in New Testament history. With the acropolis of Athens towering above, with the Epicurean and Stoic philosophers for an audience, Paul told the people of Athens something new — a God who created the universe, a God who does not dwell in temples made with hands, not even in the Parthenon.

Let's visit some of these temples that Paul saw — temples that were already 500 years old when Paul came to Athens.

These temples were located on the acropolis, the sacred hill that towered over the city, and the most beautiful was the Parthenon.

Dino Roussos:

This is the great temple of Parthenon. Parthenon means "virgin" because it was dedicated to Athena, the goddess of philosophy and wisdom. According to the ancient Greek mythology, Athena was born from the head of Zeus.

Bill Humble:

The Parthenon is often called the most beautiful expression of the classical Greek spirit. It was built during the golden age of Pericles, and the construction took 10 years, beginning in 447 B.C.

The Parthenon is 210 feet long and made of white Pentelic marble. It is built in the Doric style and has 46 columns that are 30 feet tall. There were no decorations inside the temple. That was the home of the goddess.

Dino Roussos:

The statue of Athena, made out of gold and ivory, was located in the heart of the temple. That's why the apostle Paul in his sermon to the ancient Athenians said, "God does not dwell in temples made with hands, but in him we live and breath and have our being."

Bill Humble:

Greek temples were decorated on the outside where the people gathered to worship the god or goddess. The pediments at either end of the Parthenon were decorated by the famous sculptor Pheidias. These sculptures were stripped off in 1812 and taken to the British Museum in London.

When we try to visualize the Parthenon with these sculptures in place on the two pediments, we catch a glimpse of the glory of Athens as Paul saw it.

In 437 B.C., the year after the Parthenon was completed, Pericles began work on a new monumental gateway leading up onto the acropolis. The Greek name for this gateway is *propylaea.* The earlier gateway had been destroyed in the Persian invasion forty years earlier.

The *propylaea* was over 200 feet long. It had Doric columns that supported a great marble roof. Like the Parthenon, the columns were tapered, a little larger at the bottom than at the top, and this is what gave those Greek temples their beautiful symmetry.

Caryatids at the Erechtheion in Athens.

Paul told the Athenians in his sermon that he had walked around and seen their objects of worship. So the Erechtheion was another temple that Paul must have seen. Work began on it 15 years after the Parthenon was finished. The Erechtheion was dedicated to Athena and Poseidon, the god of the sea. It was built on the spot where, according to Greek mythology, Athena and Poseidon had a contest to see which would possess Athens and protect her. Poseidon offered the sea — naval power. Athena offered the olive tree — prosperity — and won the heart of Athens. The Erechtheion was built to reconcile the two deities.

The six caryatids are the most captivating part of this temple. Extremely fine pieces of sculpture, these maidens have been holding up the great marble roof for 2,500 years.

The agora, or market place, was located at the base of the acropolis. In every Greek city the agora was the heart of city life. It was a market, or ancient shopping mall, but far more. It was where the city government was carried on, where the philosophers taught, and where citizens met to share the news.

As Paul walked around the agora, he would have seen the temple of Hephaistos, the god of fire. Built just a few years before the Parthenon, this is now the best preserved ancient temple anywhere in Greece.

On the opposite side of the agora, Paul would have wandered through the shops in the Stoa of Attalus. The stoa was reconstructed in the 1950s and serves as a museum for antiquities found in the agora.

Paul would also have seen the temple of Olympian Zeus not far from the acropolis. With 106 columns, this was the largest temple ever built in ancient Greece. The Athenians had been working on it for 500 years when Paul came to their city, and it would not be finished for another hundred years.

According to Acts 17, Paul's sermon about the unknown god was preached at the Areopagus, or Mars' Hill. Looking down from the acropolis, we see a large outcropping of rock, and this is Mars' Hill.

The oldest court in Athens met on this hill or somewhere around it in Paul's day.

When the Epicurean and Stoic philosophers heard Paul's teaching about Jesus and the resurrection, they brought him to a meeting of the Areopagus, curious to hear his "new teaching."

Today Paul's sermon is remembered in the name of the street on the south side of the acropolis — Dionysius the Areopagite street. Dionysius was one of the judges who became a believer.

Paul's sermon is also remembered in a bronze tablet on the side of Mars' Hill.

Dino Roussos:

Here we have Paul's sermon written on a bronze plaque in Koine Greek. This is how it sounded when Paul preached to the Athenians. . . . You see in the fifth line we have *agnosto theo,* "unknown god." In English you have "agnostic" and you have the word "theology," the study of God.

Bill Humble:

Athens was not the only city with an altar to unknown deities. Archaeologists found this altar in the temple of Demeter at Pergamum across the Aegean Sea from Athens. The inscription reads "To unknown gods."

It must have been a moment of high courage in Paul's life when he stood here on Mars' Hill, with the acropolis above, and told the Greek philosophers about an unknown god — a God who is found, not on the acropolis in Athens, but in an empty tomb in Jerusalem.

After preaching in Athens, Paul came here to Corinth, 50 miles to the west.

Corinth was located on a narrow isthmus between the Saronic Gulf and the Gulf of Corinth, and this gave the city one of the most strategic locations in the ancient world.

Today, the Corinth canal cuts through the isthmus. Nero tried to dig such a canal in the first century, but failed. In Paul's day there was a roadway called the *diolkos* where small ships could be dragged across the isthmus on rollers. Larger ships were unloaded, and their cargoes were carried across the isthmus to be reloaded on other ships.

Corinth had been the major city in Greece around 600 B.C. It was destroyed by the Romans in 146 B.C. and did not regain its prominence until 44 B.C., when Julius Caesar rebuilt it and made it a Roman colony. By Paul's day it was a prosperous seaport once more.

Archaeologists have been working at Corinth for nearly a hundred years, and the ruins we see are the Roman city where Paul lived and preached. It was a seaport town, very wealthy, and with all the vices that are common to such cities.

The main road leading into the city from the seaport was the Lechaion Road, and Paul probably walked on this road many times. It was lined with columns, little shops and public buildings.

One of these public buildings was the fountain of Peirene, which was a major source of Corinth's water supply. The fountain had been rebuilt by the Romans during the reign of Emperor Augustus — one of many such projects at Corinth.

Another building on the Lechaion Road housed the public toilets. Corinth may have been the first ancient city to have such public facilities.

Dino Roussos:

That's where the ancient Greek philosophers used to sit and philosophize.

Bill Humble:

The temple of Apollo was the glory of Corinth and was located on a low hill where it could be seen from all parts of the city. The temple was dedicated to Apollo, the god of music and song and poetry. It was built in the sixth century B.C., a hundred years before the Parthenon, and it was restored in the Roman rebuilding in Corinth.

Temple of Apollo at Corinth.

The temple of Apollo had 38 columns, and seven of them are still standing. These columns are different

from most Greek temples. They are monoliths — that is, each column was cut out of a single piece of stone.

At most temples the columns were put together in sections, called drums, and held in place by iron pegs. Here at the *propylaea* in Athens, it's easy to see the drums. But at the temple of Apollo each column is a single piece of stone.

Acrocorinth, the hill of Corinth, towers over the city in the distance.

The theater of Corinth was located just north of the temple of Apollo. It had been built in the fifth century B.C., then rebuilt by the Romans. Living in Corinth for a year and a half, Paul might have attended dramas and concerts here. Little remains of the theater, but sculptures that once decorated the theater are on display in the Corinth museum.

The Acrocorinth is over 1,800 feet high, and it served the city's needs in two ways. One was protection. There was a fortress on top of the mountain, and when invaders approached Corinth, the people took refuge in the fortress.

When we climb Acrocorinth and see how far it is back down to the city, we can understand why, in a thousand years, Acrocorinth was never taken by storm.

The Crusaders built a fortress on Acrocorinth, and most of the ruins we see today are Crusader. But here and there, we can see the ancient Greek walls under the Crusader ruins.

From the summit we have a beautiful view of the vineyards and fields along the Corinthian Gulf. Farming was important here in Paul's day, and this may explain why Paul used farm imagery in writing to the Corinthians — expressions like "muzzling the ox" and "plowing and threshing in hope."

But Acrocorinth served the needs of Corinth in another way. Along with the fortress, there was a temple on the summit, a temple to Aphrodite, the goddess of love. Like many a seaport town, the pleasures of Aphrodite beckoned the sailors to Corinth. This may explain why Paul preached with "fear and trembling" in Corinth.

Dino Roussos:
Why fear? Because Corinth was a very dirty, sinful city.

Bill Humble:
According to the ancient historian Strabbo, there were thousands of prostitutes who dispensed love in the temple of Aphrodite. When soldiers or merchants or sailors approached Corinth, they felt the lure of Acrocorinth where they could yield to lust in the arms of Aphrodite.

Dino Roussos:
Today the venereal diseases in the Greek language are called "aphrodisian diseases."

Bill Humble:
No wonder Paul warned the Corinthian Christians not to be united with prostitutes. And no wonder there are so many admonitions about moral purity in 1 and 2 Corinthians.

Corinth was a pagan city, but there were also Jews there. We learn from Acts that Paul preached in the synagogue every sabbath before turning to the Gentiles.

Archaeologists have found an inscription that confirms the Jewish presence in Corinth. The inscription is on a stone lintel and it reads, "Synagogue of the

Hebrews." They have also found a piece of marble decorated with three menorah. However, both of these are considerably later than the time of Paul.

Corinth had a large agora, or market place, lined with shops on all sides. One of these little shops has been restored, with its vaulted roof, to give us an idea of what they looked like. We know from Acts that Paul worked as a tentmaker with Aquila and Priscilla, and their shop might have been located here in the agora.

The Isthmian Games were held about 10 miles from Corinth, and these games gave tentmakers a ready market.

Dino Roussos:

Because of the Isthmian Games being nearby, people came from all over Greece and lived in tents. So Paul had an opportunity to make tents or to repair them and make money and support himself.

Bill Humble:

Judging from the references to boxers and runners in 1 Corinthians, Paul may have been a spectator at the Isthmian Games.

The *bema* was located on the south side of the agora. It was a large platform, covered with blue and white marble, that was used for civic affairs. The Roman governor would address the people from the *bema*. Paul might have preached here. Trials were held before the *bema,* and in Acts 18, Paul was the accused.

Dino Roussos:

They brought Paul right here to the judgment seat. Gallio was sitting right on the top of this *bema*. Paul was right in front of the judgment seat on this little pillar where they used to chain the criminals.

Bill Humble:

This historic little pillar is where the accused stood, often in chains, to be tried. But as Paul stood here, Governor Gallio realized that it was a religious dispute among the Jews, so he refused to have anything to do with it. And Acts says that the people turned on Sosthenes, the ruler of the synagogue, and beat him in front of the *bema.*

Dino Roussos:

Sosthenes was the ruler of the synagogue here in Corinth where Paul came and preached, and here we have the name Sosthenes.

Bill Humble:

The name Sosthenes is still legible on this monument.

There is another inscription, still in place, that relates to one of Paul's friends.

Paul wrote the book of Romans from Corinth, and in the last chapter he sent greetings to the Roman church from Erastus, "the city treasurer," he is called. In 1929 archaeologists found this inscription in Corinth. It says, "Erastus laid this pavement at his own expense." Erastus was a sort of county commissioner here in Corinth, and archaeologists believe that this Erastus is the same man who was a friend of Paul and sent greetings to the church in Rome.

Here's another inscription that has two familiar New Testament names on it: Cornelius and Theophilus. No, these are not the men we read about in Acts. But it is interesting that this Cornelius, at Corinth, was called "Theophilus," a friend of God.

At a site like Corinth, it is easy to see the value of archaeology for New Testament studies.

Dino Roussos:

Archaeology has brought to light all these ancient Greek cities where Paul lived and worked and preached and started New Testament churches. What the book of Acts writes about Paul's missionary journey is true. So the Bible is not a mythological book, but it's very historic and authentic and true.

Bill Humble:

Here at Corinth we see one of the great values of archaeology for the Bible. This is the Corinth that Paul knew. These are the streets where he walked, the buildings he passed day after day for a year and a half. Here at Corinth we share Paul's life. We live in the world where he lived. And this is one of the great values of archaeology — to give us a picture window into that world that Paul knew.

Scriptures for Study

Acts 17:16-34. Paul's sermon at Mars' Hill.

Acts 18:1-21. Paul's ministry at Corinth.

Romans 16:23. Erastus.

1 Corinthians 5:1-13; 6:12-20. Warnings against immorality.

Notes from Archaeology

The Parthenon

The Parthenon is never mentioned in the New Testament except in Paul's reference at Mars' Hill to his passing along and beholding the objects of their worship at Athens (Acts 17:23). But Paul must have gazed in wonder at the beauty of the Parthenon — the most perfect monument of the classical Greek spirit — just as millions of tourists do today.

The Parthenon was built between 447 B.C. and 438 B.C. during the "golden age of Pericles." The Parthenon is 228 feet long, 111 feet wide, and 60 feet high. It is built in the Doric style, of white Pentelic marble, and has 46 fluted columns. The sculpture reliefs (pediments) on the two ends were done by Phidias under the direction of Pericles, and are some of the most perfect expressions of Greek art. The eastern pediment showed the birth of Athena from the head of Zeus. The western pediment pictured the contest between Athena and Poseidon to see which one would possess Athens. The metopes, sculptures on the two sides, were of the struggles between men and their mythological enemies.

The only art inside the Parthenon was a 40-foot-high statue of Athena. It, too, was done by Phidias. It was made of wood covered with gold and ivory — gold for Athena's clothing and ivory for flesh.

The Parthenon has a subtle architecture that gave it the perfect symmetry and proportion admired across the ages. To achieve this symmetry, the architects Ictinus and Callicrates did not have a single straight line or perfectly perpendicular wall or column anywhere in the building. Since the human eye tends to see a slight dip in a straight line, the floors and steps in the Parthenon all have a slight curve to counteract this optical illusion. The curve is ever so slight — the curve of a circle with a 3½-mile radius — but it makes the floors and steps appear straight. But when one gets down and sights along the steps, the slight curve can be seen.

Similarly, perfectly perpendicular columns appear to be falling apart to the human eye. Therefore the

Parthenon columns are tapered, a little smaller at the top. The tapering is so slight that if the lines of the two end columns were extended skyward, they would converge one-and-a-half miles above the earth. But this slight tapering was just enough to give the Parthenon its remarkable symmetry and beauty.

The Parthenon served as a Greek temple to Diana for 900 years. During the Byzantine period, it was transformed into a church honoring the Virgin Mary and this use continued for 1,000 years. For the next two centuries it was a Muslim mosque. Remarkably well-preserved for over 2,000 years, the Parthenon was partially destroyed in a war in 1687. The Turks were using it as a powder magazine when a shell hit it and set off a destructive explosion. The final desecration came in 1812 when Lord Elgin stripped off the surviving sculptures and carried them to London, where they are now displayed in the British Museum.

The Greeks have now undertaken a major restoration of the Parthenon. And there is a full-scale replica of the Parthenon in Centennial Park in Nashville, Tenn.

Even after suffering the ravages of war, the Parthenon still has a captivating beauty. But undaunted by its ancient beauty, Paul courageously told the Athenians about the true God, a God who is not found in the beautiful Parthenon but in an empty tomb in Jerusalem.

A Prosperous, Sinful City

Corinth was blessed with one of the most strategic locations anywhere in the ancient world. It was on the narrow isthmus that connected southern Greece, called the Peloponnesus, with the cities of northern

Greece — Athens, Delphi and Philippi. The isthmus was also the gateway for sea trade between the Saronic Gulf to the east and the Gulf of Corinth on the west, so Corinth had two seaports, Cenchrea (Acts 18:18; Romans 16:1) on the Saronic Gulf and Lechaeum on the Gulf of Corinth. Because of this strategic location, Corinth was in a position to control land commerce between northern and southern Greece and sea traffic from east and west. Corinth had become, in Paul's day, the most prosperous city in all Greece.

If ships did not stop at Corinth, they faced a 200-mile-long sea voyage around Cape Malea at the south tip of Greece. This voyage was so dangerous and the winds so treacherous that an old Greek proverb warned, "When you go around Cape Malea, forget your home." Instead of risking the dangers of Malea, ship owners found it prudent to sail to one of Corinth's ports, unload their cargo, and transport it across the four-mile-wide isthmus, to be reloaded on other vessels at the opposite port.

In the sixth century B.C., the *diolkos* was built to transport smaller ships across the isthmus without having to unload them. The *diolkos* was a stone roadway. Smaller vessels were taken out of the water, dragged across the *diolkos* on roller-like skids, and then launched again at the opposite port. Remains of the *diolkos* still survive and have been uncovered by archaeologists.

The *diolkos* was still in use during the years that Paul lived in Corinth. But a few years later, in 66 A.D., the Emperor Nero tried to dig a canal across the isthmus. Nero himself moved the first earth with a golden shovel. However, the canal proved too difficult an undertaking for Nero's day. Less than a hundred years ago, in 1893, the present Corinth canal was completed. The canal is 4½ miles long, 250 feet deep at the deepest point, and the water is 25 feet deep.

Thanks to its command of the trade routes, Corinth was the most prosperous city in Greece in Paul's day. But at the same time, it had all the vices of a seaport city and was the most notorious seat of immorality anywhere in the Roman world. The Temple of Aphrodite, goddess of love, towered over the city on the Acrocorinth. The first-century Greek author Strabo has reported in his *Geography* that a thousand temple prostitutes served the travelers and sailors who came to Aphrodite. While some have questioned Strabo's credibility, there is no doubt that Corinth was notorious for its sin, immorality and prostitution.

No wonder that Paul preached in Corinth with fear and trembling.

No wonder that his two letters have so many warnings about prostitution and immorality.

No wonder the church Paul left in Corinth faced serious problems in a city where sin was so pervasive.

The Bema

The *bema,* located in the *agora* at Corinth, is of special biblical interest because Paul once stood before the *bema,* the accused in a trial before Governor Gallio. In all Greek cities the *agora* was the "town square" and served many purposes. Surrounded by shops, the *agora* was an ancient shopping mall, the city's civic center, and a meeting place where the populace exchanged news.

At Corinth the *bema,* a large stone platform covered with white and blue marble, stood on the south side of the *agora.* The *bema* was used for many civic functions. When Roman governors needed to address the people, they assembled in the *agora* and the governor spoke from the *bema*. An inscription from Corinth states that certain proclamations were read from the *bema*. It is possible that Paul might have preached Christ from the *bema*. Trials were sometimes held at the *bema*. The judges sat on the *bema*, and the prisoner, often in chains, stood at a small column in front of the *bema*.

Toward the end of his 18-month ministry at Corinth, Paul was the accused at such a trial (Acts 18:12-18). The Jews brought Paul before Governor Gallio and charged that he was "persuading men to worship God contrary to the law." The word *bema* occurs in the Greek text three times. They brought Paul before the *bema* (v. 12), Gallio drove them from the *bema* (v. 16), and they beat Sosthenes in front of the *bema* (v. 17). Our English Bibles translate *bema* as "judgment seat" (KJV) or "tribunal" (RSV).

When Governor Gallio realized that the Jews' charges against Paul were a religious dispute and did not involve Roman law, he refused to consider the case and "drove them from the *bema*." Whereupon, some spectators seized Sosthenes, the ruler of the synagogue, and beat him in front of the *bema*. An inscription has been found in the excavations at Corinth that has the name of Sosthenes on it.

At Delphi archaeologists found an inscription with Gallio's name on it and the date when he began serving as governor at Corinth. This inscription is important for New Testament chronology. It places Paul's ministry at Corinth during the years 51-52 A.D., and this, in turn, becomes a fixed date in working out the dating for all of Paul's life and missionary journeys.

Erastus

Paul wrote the book of Romans from Corinth and included greetings from many Corinthian Christians to the church in Rome. One of these was "Erastus, the city treasurer" (Romans 16:23).

In 1929 archaeologists found an inscription on a pavement in a small plaza near the Corinth theater. The name Erastus was in the inscription. The letters of the inscription had been incised in paving stones of gray Acrocorinthian limestone and then inlaid with bronze. Most of the bronze inlay has disappeared, but the letters cut into the limestone are still easily legible. The inscription says, "Erastus in return for the aedileship laid [the pavement] at his own expense." The *aedile* was a public official at Corinth, a sort of "director of public works" or "county commissioner" in charge of streets and public buildings. The inscription has been dated to 50-100 A.D., and since Erastus was not a common name, scholars think that this Erastus who is honored in the inscription is the same man who sent greetings to the Roman church in Romans 16:23.

The name Erastus is found in two other New Testament passages. In Acts 19:22 Paul sent "two of his helpers, Timothy and Erastus," into Macedonia, while he remained in Ephesus to finish his three-year ministry there. But since this was only a short time before Paul went on to Corinth, where he wrote Romans, this helper named Erastus can hardly have been the "city treasurer" in Corinth. There is a final reference to Paul's co-worker in 2 Timothy 4:20: "Erastus remained at Corinth."

Printed in the United States
1425700004B/7-15